I0704981

PSYCHOLOGICAL OPERATIONS IN GUERRILLA WARFARE

Introduction by Emanuel Pietrobon

Design by Elham Makdoum

CONTENTS

Past, present and future of psychological warfare

By Emanuel Pietrobon

It is sometimes possible to change the attitudes of millions but impossible to change the attitude of one man.

Edward Bernays

Since the dawn of Man, the mind has been the battlefield, and psychological manipulation has been the refuge and subterfuge of cunning strategists who, though poor in resources but rich in genius, overwhelm or attempt to overwhelm the predictability of convention with the destructive chaos of creativity.

Psychological wars are the engine of history. It was by persuading Adam and Eve to break the inviolable prohibition against eating from the Tree of Knowledge of Good and Evil that Satan exacted his revenge for the defeat suffered in a previous conventional war against the angelic armies of his Creator. It was by filling the battlefield with cats that the Persians defeated their superstitious Egyptian adversaries in the Battle of Pelusium. It was by emptying his own fortresses that the skillful Cáo Cāo repeatedly forced the retreat of the numerically superior troops of the powerful but naive Lü Bu, who was induced by reverse psychology to believe that traps and ambushes had been set in those abandoned sites. It was by lining the road to Wallachia with beheaded and impaled bodies that Vlad Ţepeş repeatedly triumphed over his enemies, the Ottomans, who were technologically and numerically superior but psychologically paralyzed. It was by forging the Bryce Report that the British Empire manipulated the feelings of Western public opinion, particularly that of the United States, inculcating in them the belief that the soldiers of Wilhelm II were committing atrocities and war crimes around the world. It was by reproducing the screams of possessed people, ghostly voices, and bestial sounds through hidden loudspeakers in the jungle, rigorously activated in the dead of night, that U.S. soldiers deprived the Viet Cong of sleep, leading the most superstitious to abandon their positions[1].

Psychology can be a weapon of mass construction or (mass) destruction, depending on the objective of the person using it. Political communication, advertising, war propaganda and mind-centric operations are the four faces of the psychological Brahma. Political communication to manufacture consensus and/or to demolish the reputation of the contender in times of

---

1   Operation Wandering Soul.

elections and government. Advertising to induce in consumers needs that they do not need. War propaganda to mobilize one's own people and to demoralize those of the enemy. Mind-centric operations of cognitive type to open an internal front to the adversary, a front corresponding to a society in liquefaction or boiling, or of psychological or informational type to destabilize and disinform.

From the expulsion of Adam and Eve to the present day, when wars are waged online, nothing has changed: the mind is still an invisible trench where battles of words and images are fought and are capable of, and aim to, producing reverberations in the real world. This is why the study of Carl von Clausewitz should be accompanied by that of Edward Bernays and the many fathers of wars for the dominion of the mind. This is why MasiraX has decided to publish the most controversial manual on psychological warfare of the twentieth century: Psychological Operations in Guerrilla Warfare.

What you have in your hands is a handbook on how to produce instability and violence in fragile sociopolitical contexts, which indeed generated instability and violence in one of the most fragile (and most contested) sociopolitical contexts of the Cold War: Nicaragua in the 1980s.

Developed by a counterinsurgency specialist of the Central Intelligence Agency (CIA) whose identity has never been revealed[2], this handbook was originally published in English and Spanish and was distributed among Nicaraguan counterrevolutionaries in early 1984.

It was the final stages of the Cold War, the decisive stages, which saw the Soviet Union under pressure in Poland and Afghanistan, two theaters in which the United States was applying the geopolitics of faith with exceptional results, and the only thing left to disturb the sleep of the optimist Ronald Reagan was a small and unsuspected state: Nicaragua. Since a reedition of Urgent Fury[3] was not feasible—partly due to the memory of the failure of the early 20th-century American occupation and partly because Poland and Afghanistan required maximum attention—the White House opted for the conduct of a high-intensity covert war.

Power in strategic Nicaragua had been assumed by a revolutionary force ideologically aligned with the Second World, which harked back to the thinking of Augusto César Sandino[4], to which the United States had responded by assembling a conglomerate popularly known as the Contras, short for *Contrarrevolucionarios* (lit. Counterrevolutionaries), made up of

---

2   The author of the manual was granted the right of anonymity, which continues to this day. John Kirkpatrick, the name that appears in the original edition, is only an alias.

3   Invasion of Grenada.

4   Sandino was the charismatic leader of an armed resistance movement to the American occupation of Nicaragua, active between 1927 and 1932, and has since been revered as a national hero.

loyalists of the defunct dictatorship, right-wing extremists, criminals and mercenaries. Nomen omen: the Contras indeed represented the counterrevolution, they were the antithesis of Sandinismo, and from a heterogeneous and unlikely coalition of the willing set up by Washington, involving sworn enemies such as Tel Aviv[5], Riyadh[6] and Tehran[7] and such as Beijing[8] and Taipei[9], they were receiving everything necessary to prevent the maturation of a second Cuba in the Americas. The world against Sandino's shadow.

At a certain point in 1983, recognizing the underwhelming results of the escalation, Reagan tasked the CIA with developing a supplement to integrate into the guerrilla warfare. He felt that something was missing—and he was right: the Contras operation was all weapons and no psychology.

Psychology, which had been the key to the success of the covert wars against Mohammad Mossadeq's Iran[10], against Jacobo Árbenz's Guatemala[11] and against Salvador Allende's Chile[12], had

---

5 Jonathan Marshall, *Israel, the Contras and the North Trial*, MERIP, September/October 1989.
6 Doyle McManus, *Contras May Have Got $30 Million From Saudi Arabia*, Los Angeles Times, January 15, 1987.
7 Iran-Contra scandal.
8 Jack Anderson, Dale van Atta, *Red China Sell Arms to Contras*, The Washington Post, May 5, 1986.
9 *Taiwan Says It Did Provide Aid to Contras*, Los Angeles Times, May 16, 1987.
10 Operation Ajax.
11 Operation PBSUCCESS.
12 Operation FUBELT.

incredibly found no place in Nicaragua. Given the high popularity of the Sandinistas, the risk was that the Contras operation could turn out to be a debacle, much like Operation Mongoose[13]. It couldn't happen. Not again. Not now that the United States had the Soviet Union in its grip and was on the brink of victory.

> Every group, every club, every society has its leading
> Pavlovian Bell.
>
> Joost A. M. Meerloo

The Contras knew the territory in which they were fighting, had been trained in the art of asymmetric warfare, and were supported militarily and economically by an international coalition. Nevertheless, they were unable to expand the territories under their control or to gain the sympathy of their fellow countrymen.

This manual was written and made a mandatory study text

---

13 Mongoose is the name of a subversive operation through which the United States attempted to undermine the stability of the Cuban communist regime during the 1960s, entrusting American Mafia elements, mercenaries, and CIA saboteurs with the task of carrying out attacks against strategic infrastructures and political targets. CIA analysts were convinced that Castroism did not enjoy popular support and that the wave of artificial terror would encourage Cubans to rebel. This was not the case: the vast majority of Cubans were enthusiastic about the new political order and, contrary to the analysts' predictions, responded to the instability by rallying even more tightly around the Castros.

in the training camps of the anti-Sandinistas to address the Contras' near-total lack of knowledge of psychology. The goal: to apply the teachings of individual and group psychology to guerrilla warfare, or in the words of its author, to transform the Contras from mere fighters into "propagandist fighters", from saboteurs into "agitators".

The Contras had the weapons to pierce the bodies of the Sandinistas, but they did not have the tools to win the hearts and minds of the Nicaraguans. The CIA compendium aimed to fill this gap, drawing on Bernays, Hubert Lyautey, Ivan Pavlov and Wilfred Trotter to refine and discipline these crude guerrillas who, with their senseless and indiscriminate violence against civilians, victims of torture and rape, were discrediting and mudslinging Reagan's small crusade for freedom in Nicaragua. And they had caused the opening of a historic and spectacular trial against the United States at the International Court of Justice[14].

The anonymous CIA counterinsurgency specialist hiding behind the pseudonym Kirkpatrick had been given a pedagogical mission with political implications. His manual was supposed to explain to the Contras "how to build political support in Nicaragua through deception, intimidation and violence", that is, how to expand the battlefield from the jungle to the cities by

---

14 The story of the International Court of Justice case "Nicaragua v. United States" has been told in:
Emanuel Pietrobon, *L'arte della guerra ibrida. Teoria e prassi della destabilizzazione*, Castelvecchi, 2022.

enlisting the most vulnerable, and therefore most manipulable, segments of society in the tête-à-tête.

The (long) history of psychological warfare, which with the advent of the Internet and the global village have evolved into cognitive, shows that Pavlov's theory of behavior conditioning is equally applicable to canines and humans. Meerloo, the theorist of menticide, argued that every person and every group have an Achilles heel. A researcher must do nothing but find it, investigate it and hit it with the arrow of psychology.

No one is immune to emotional manipulation. Everyone is a potential Manchurian candidate. A small farmer can be encouraged to take up arms against the government he loves by waving the prospect of land reform, a woman can be brought to protest by exploiting the underlying intolerance towards patriarchal society, discriminated minorities can be encouraged to rebel by fanning their discontent and promising them change. Psychological warfare is the field of the possible, because it can awaken powerful feelings and emotions that have been buried and put to sleep by layers of the unconscious.

This handbook could have been published at eleven fifty-nine yesterday evening. The passage of time has not negatively affected the validity of its contents, which remain tremendously current. Because the techniques for behavioral manipulation and mental influence of individuals and masses, in times of peace and in times of war, open or covert, are basically always the same. Don't make the grave mistake of believing that technological progress has made tactics such as entryism[15], demoralization, and intimidation obsolete. The opposite is true: the media and persuasive technologies have amplified the destabilizing charge of psychological operations, while the world-turned-global village is a guarantee of virality. Yesterday a hoax could reach its target through clandestine printing, illegal radio or flyers dropped from airplanes, today it can go around the world in a minute with a click.

Technological progress and changes in the media system have not led to the extinction of anything, but to the evolution of everything. Cartoons have become memes. Propaganda has become storytelling. Social media are the new town squares. Influencers are the new priests. The changes have occurred in form, not content; therefore these pages retain a vivid topicality.

By publishing this manual, which has been enriched with other material on the covert war in Nicaragua, the MasiraX team wants to offer a high-level educational service to its community, which is made up of both students of political, security and historical issues and professionals, in the awareness that a reading of this kind can make the difference between an autonomous person and an automaton.

---

15 Infiltration of agents of influence and provocateurs into a movement that one wants to destabilize from within.

Intended to be the inaugural issue of *PsyWars*, a series entirely dedicated to propaganda and the many faces of wars for the mind, this manual and the works that will follow, if understood rather than merely read, can help you become that manipulation-proof individual that Bernays spoke of.

Be jealous of your Pavlovian bell.

1936. The Somozas create a family-based dictatorship in Nicaragua with the approval of the United States.

1956. President Anastasio Somoza is assassinated. He is succeeded by his son Luis.

1961. The Sandinista National Liberation Front is founded, marking the beginning of an increasingly violent civil war.

1967. President Luis Somoza dies of a heart attack. He is succeeded by his brother Anastasio.

1979. The Sandinistas put President Somoza to flight. He finds refuge abroad. They establish a revolutionary junta.

1980. The Sandinistas kill the former president in Asunción, Paraguay.

1981. The United States begins secretly selling weapons to Iran, then under embargo, as part of a scheme to raise funds for the armed opposition to the Sandinista government, the Contras.

1983. The Central Intelligence Agency asks to one of its analysts, operating under the pseudonyms John Kirkpatrick and Tayacán, to write a manual on psychological warfare for the Contras.

1984. The handbook, titled Psychological Operations in Guerrilla Warfare, is secretly distributed in Nicaragua.

1986. The Nicaraguan government files a lawsuit against the United States in the International Court of Justice, holding them responsible for the Contra uprising and presenting a copy of Psychological Operations in Guerrilla Warfare as evidence. The International Court of Justice rules in favor of Nicaragua and orders the United States to cease undeclared hostilities.

1990. Return to normalcy: the anti-Sandinista armed opposition disappears, new elections.

PREFACE

Guerrilla warfare is essentially a political war. For this reason, its area of operations goes beyond the territorial limits of conventional warfare, penetrating the political being "par excellence" itself: the "political animal" defined by Aristoteles[16].

In effect, the human being must be considered as the priority objective in a political war. And viewed as the military target of guerrilla warfare, the most critical point of the human being is the mind. Once the mind has been reached, the "political animal" has been vanquished, without necessarily having received any shots.

Guerrilla warfare emerges and grows in a political environment; in the constant struggle to dominate that area of the political mentality which is inherent in every human being, and which collectively constitutes the "environment" in which guerrilla warfare moves, and which is precisely the arena in which its triumph or defeat is defined.

This concept of guerrilla warfare as a political war turns Psychological Operations into the factor that determines the results. The target, then, are the minds of the population, the entire population: our troops, the enemy troops, and the civil population.

---

16 According to Aristoteles, "man is by nature a political animal".

This book is a guerrilla training manual for Psychological Operations, and it is applied to the specific case of the Christian and democratic crusade being conducted in Nicaragua by the Freedom Commandos.

Welcome!

I.   INTRODUCTION

1. <u>General Background</u>

The aim of this book is to introduce the guerrilla student to psychological operation techniques, which will have an immediate and practical value in guerrilla warfare. This section is introductory and general in nature; the following sections will cover every point mentioned here in more detail.

The nature of the environment in guerrilla warfare does not allow sophisticated psychological operations, and it becomes necessary for the group, detachment and squadron leaders to carry out, with minimum direction from the upper echelons, psychological action operations with the contacts who know the reality from the roots.

2. <u>Propagandist Combatant Guerrillas</u>

In order to obtain the maximum results from psychological operation in guerrilla warfare, each combatant must be highly motivated to engage in propaganda face to face, to the same degree he is motivated to fight. This means that the guerrilla's individual political awareness, the reason for his struggle, must be as acute as his capacity to fight.

Such a degree of political awareness and motivation is obtained through group dynamics and self-criticism as a standard teaching method for guerrilla training and operations. Group discussions increase the spirit and the unity of thought of guerrilla squadrons, and they exert social pressure on the weaker members to perform a better role in future training or in combat actions. Self-criticism is made in terms of one's own contribution or failures in one's contribution to the cause, the movement, the struggle, etc., and this introduces an element of positive individual commitment to the mission of the group.

The desired result is a guerrilla soldier who may justify his actions persuasively when he is in contact with any member of the Nicaraguan People, and especially to himself and his guerrilla companions when enduring the vicissitudes of guerrilla warfare. This means that each guerrilla will be persuasive in face-to-face communication—propagandist & combatant—and in his contact with the people; he must be capable of giving 5 or 10 logical reasons why, for example, a peasant must give him fabric, needle and thread to mend his clothes.

When the guerrilla behaves this way, enemy propaganda will never turn him into an enemy in the eyes of the population. It also means that hunger, cold, fatigue and insecurity will have a meaning, psychologically, in the struggle for the cause, because of constant orientation.

3. <u>Armed Propaganda</u>

Armed propaganda includes every action performed, and the good impression which this armed force may give will result in the population having a positive attitude towards those forces; it does not include forced indoctrination. Armed propaganda improves the behavior of the population towards its author, and it is not achieved by force.

This means that an armed guerrilla unit in a rural town will not give the impression that its weapons are a force that they hold over the peasants, but rather that they are the strength of the peasants against the repressive Sandinista government. This is achieved through a close identification with the population, as follows: hanging up the weapons and working alongside them in their fields, in construction, harvesting the grain, fishing, etc.; giving explanations to young men about basic weapons, for example, giving them an unloaded weapon and allowing them to touch it, see it, etc., giving a basic description of its operation; describing, with simple slogans, how the weapons will serve the people in winning their freedom; adopting the demands of the people for hospitals and education, a reduction of taxes, etc.

The objective of all these actions is to create an identification of the people with the weapons and with the guerrillas who carry them, so that the population feels that those weapons are, indirectly, the weapons that will protect them and help them in their struggle against an oppressive regime. There is always implicit terror in weapons, since the people are internally "aware" that they could be used against them; however, as long as explicit coercion can be avoided, we may achieve positive attitudes about the presence of armed guerrillas in the midst of the population.

4. <u>Armed Propaganda Teams</u>

Armed Propaganda Teams (EPA, *Equipos de Propaganda Armada*) are constituted through a careful selection of persuasive and highly motivated guerrillas, moving within the population, motivating the people to support the guerrillas and resist the enemy. They combine a high degree of political awareness and guerrillas' capacity for armed propaganda, towards a planned, controlled and programmed effort.

The careful selection of personnel, based on their persuasive powers in informal discussions and on their combat capability, is more important than the level of their education or than the training program. The Armed Propaganda Team's tactics must be carried out covertly, and they must be parallel to the tactical efforts in guerrilla warfare. Knowledge of the psychology of the population is a primary necessity for the Armed

Propaganda Teams, but much more intelligence data will be obtained from an EPA program in the area of operations.

5. Development and Control of "Front" Organizations

The development and control of "front" organizations is carried out through internal subjective (concealed) control, through group meetings of the "internal cadres", and by calculating the time needed for the combination of these two elements to be applied to the masses.

Established citizens—doctors, attorneys, businessmen, teachers, etc.—will be recruited initially as "Social Crusaders" in typically "innocuous" movements in the area of operations. When their "involvement" with the clandestine organization is revealed to them, this exerts psychological pressure on them so that they can be used as "internal cadres" in groups to which they already belong or groups which they could join.

Then, through a gradual and skillful process, they will receive instruction in persuasion techniques for the control of target groups which will support our democratic revolution. A system for the control of cells isolates individuals from one another, and at the appropriate moment, their influence is used to fuse the groups together into a united national front.

6. <u>Control of Meetings and Mass Assemblies</u>

The control of mass meetings in support of guerrilla warfare is carried out internally through a covert commando element, bodyguards, messengers, shock troops (incident initiators), poster carriers (also used to give signals), and slogan shouters, all under the control of the external commando element.

When the cadres are placed in or recruited from organizations such as labor unions, youth groups, agricultural organizations or professional associations, they will begin to manipulate the groups' objectives. The psychological apparatus of our movement, by means of these internal cadres, will prepare a mental attitude which, at the crucial moment, could become involved in a fury of justified violence.

This can be carried out through a small group of guerrillas infiltrated within the masses, who will have the mission of agitating, giving the impression that there are many of them and that they have great popular support. Using the tactics of a force of 200 to 300 agitators, one can create a demonstration in which 10,000 to 20,000 could take part.

7. <u>Support from Contacts Who are Rooted in Reality</u>

The support of local contacts who know reality down to its

roots is achieved through the exploitation of the social and political weaknesses of the target society, with propagandist-combatant guerrillas, armed propaganda, armed propaganda teams, front organizations and mass meetings.

The propagandist-combatant guerrilla is the result of a constant program of indoctrination and motivation. They will have the mission of demonstrating to the people the greatness and the justice of our movement, to all Nicaraguans and to the world. By identifying with our people, sympathy toward our movement will increase, which will result in greater support from the population towards the freedom commandos, taking away sympathy from the regime in power.

Armed propaganda will extend this process of identification with the Christian guerrillas, providing [an awareness of] common traits against the Sandinista regime.

The Armed Propaganda Teams provide a stage-by-stage persuasive planning program in all areas of the country. These teams are also the "eyes and ears" of our movement.

The development and control of front organizations in guerrilla warfare will give our movement the ability to create the effect of a "whip" within the population, when the order to merge is given. When infiltration and subjective internal control have developed parallel to other guerrilla activities, one of our commanders will be able to literally shake down the Sandinista structure and replace it.

The meetings and mass assemblies are the culmination of a broad base of support among the population, and they occur in the later phases of the operation. This is the moment in which an overthrow may be achieved and our revolution can come out in the open, requiring the close collaboration of the entire population of the country, and requiring contacts who are rooted in reality.

Tactical effort in guerrilla warfare is directed at the enemy's weaknesses, and toward destroying their military capability to resist, and must go parallel with a psychological effort to weaken and destroy their sociopolitical capability at the same time. In guerrilla warfare, more than in any other type of military effort, psychological activities must take place simultaneously with military activities, in order to achieve the desired objectives.

II.   PROPAGANDIST-COMBATANT GUERRILLA

1. General Background

The objective of this section is to familiarize the guerrilla with psychological operation techniques, which maximizes the social psychological effect of a guerrilla movement, turning the guerrilla into a propagandist, in addition to a combatant. The nature of the guerrilla warfare environment does not allow sophisticated facilities to conduct psychological operations; for this reason, we must make use of each guerrilla's effective face-to-face persuasion.

2. Political Awareness

The guerrilla's individual political awareness, the reason for his struggle, shall be as important as his ability to fight. This motivation of political awareness will be achieved by:

Improving the guerrilla's combat potential by increasing his motivation to fight.

- Recognizing the guerrilla as a vital link between the democratic guerrilla and the support of the people, essential to the subsistence of both.

- Promoting the support of the population for the national

insurgency [movement] through the support of the local guerrillas, which provides a psychological base in the population for [participation in] politics, after the achievement of victory.

– Developing trust in the guerrillas and the population for the reconstruction of the local and national government.

– Promoting the value of guerrilla and popular participation in the civic affairs of the insurrection and in the national programs.

– Developing in each guerrilla the capability for face-to-face persuasion on the local level, in order to gain the support of the population, which is a key element for the success of the guerrilla warfare.

3. <u>Group Dynamics</u>

This political awareness and motivation is obtained using group dynamics at the level of small units. The group discussion method and self-criticism are general techniques for training and guerrilla operations.

Group discussions increase the [group] spirit and a unity of thought in small guerrilla groups, and exert social pressure on the weaker members, so that they may better carry out their mission in future training and combat action. These group discussions will place particular emphasis on:

- Creating an opinion favorable to our movement. Using the national and local history, making it understood that the Sandinista regime is "foreign", "repressive" and "imperialistic", and although there are some Nicaraguans within the government, we will make it evident that they are power "puppets" of the Soviets and the Cubans, that is, foreign powers.

- Always a local approach. Matters of an international nature will be explained only as support for local events in guerrilla warfare.

- Our goal is the unification of the nation. This means that the defeat of the armed Sandinista forces is our priority. Our insurrectional movement is a pluralist political platform, from which we are determined to win liberty, equality, a better economy with opportunities to work, a higher level of living and a true democracy for all Nicaraguans without exception.

- Providing each guerrilla with a clear understanding about the struggle for national sovereignty against Soviet-Cuban imperialism. Discussion guides will lead the guerrillas to see the injustices of the Sandinista regime.

- Demonstrating to each guerrilla the need for good behavior in order to win the support of the population. The discussion guides must convince the guerrillas that the attitude and opinion of the population is a determining factor, because victory is impossible without popular support.

— Self-criticism will take place in constructive terms that will contribute to the mission of the movement, and that will provide the guerrillas with the certainty that they have the constant and positive individual responsibility in the group mission. The method for instruction shall be:

a) Divide the guerrilla force into squadrons for group discussions, including command and support elements, as long as the tactical situation allows it. The integrity of the small units must be maintained when these groups are designed.

b) Assign a political cadre in the guerrilla force to each group, to guide the discussion. The squadron leader must help the cadre to promote the study and the expression of thoughts. If there aren't enough political cadres for each squadron or detachment, the leaders must guide the discussions, and the available cadres must visit groups alternately.

c) The cadre (or the leader) should guide the group discussion in order to cover a number of points and reach a correct conclusion. The guerrillas must feel that they have made their own free decision. The cadre must act like a tutor. The cadre or leader will not act like a lecturer, but rather will help the members of the groups to study and express their own opinions.

d) At the end of each discussion, the political cadre will make a summary of the principal points, taking them to the correct conclusions. Any serious differences with the objectives of the movement must be noted by the cadre and reported to the commander of the forces. If necessary, a meeting of the combined groups will be held, and the team of political cadres will explain and clear up the misunderstanding.

e) Democratic conduct on the part of the political cadres: living, eating and working with the guerrillas, and, if possible, fighting at their side, sharing their living conditions. All of this will propitiate understanding and a spirit of cooperation which will help in the discussion and exchange of ideas.

f) Holding group discussions in towns, and in areas of operation with civil populations, whenever possible, and not limiting them to the camps or bases. This is done in order to emphasize the revolutionary nature of the struggle and to demonstrate that the guerrillas identified with the objectives of the people move within the population. The guerrilla is focused toward the people, like the political cadre is toward the guerrilla, and they must live, eat and work together in order to achieve unity of revolutionary thought.

The principles for the groups discussions between guerrillas and political cadres are:

– Organize discussion groups at the detachment or squadron level. A cadre cannot be certain of comprehension and understanding of the concepts and conclusions on the part of the guerrillas in large groups. In a group the size of a 10-man squadron, judgment and control of the situation are greater. This way, all the students will participate in an exchange among them, the political leader, the leader of the group, and also the political cadre. Special attention will be given to the individual ability to discuss the objectives of the insurrectional struggle. When a guerrilla expresses his opinion, he will be interested in hearing the opinions of others, and this will result in unity of thought.

- Combine the different points of view and reach a common judgment or conclusion. This is the most difficult task for a political cadre in the guerrilla. After the group discussions about the democratic objectives of the movement, the leader of the team of political cadres of the guerrilla force must combine the conclusions of the individual groups into a general summary. In a meeting with all the discussion groups, the cadre will provide the main points, and the guerrillas will have the opportunity to clarify or modify their viewpoints. In order to do this, the conclusions will be summarized as slogans, whenever possible.

- Honestly face the national and local problems of our struggle. The political cadres must always be prepared to discuss solutions to the problems observed by the guerrillas. During the discussions, the guerrillas must be guided by the following three principles:
    - Loyalty of thought.
    - Freedom of expression.
    - Concentration of thoughts towards the objectives of the democratic struggle.

The result desired is that a guerrilla may persuasively justify all his actions whenever he is in contact with any member of the people, and especially to himself and his fellow guerrillas, while enduring the vicissitudes of guerrilla warfare.

- This means that each guerrilla will be able to conduct effective face-to-face persuasion as a propagandist-combatant in his contact with the people, to the point of being able to give 5 or 10 logical reasons why, for example, a peasant should give him a piece of fabric, or needle and thread to mend his clothes. When a guerrilla behaves like this, no kind of enemy propaganda will be able to make him a "terrorist" in the eyes of the people.

- Thus, even the hunger, cold, fatigue and insecurity in the existence of a guerrilla, will acquire meaning in the struggle for the cause, due to the constant psychological orientation.

4. <u>Camp Procedures</u>

Camping gives greater motivation to guerrilla units, in addition to reducing distractions and increasing the spirit of cooperation of the small units, relating the physical environment with the psychological atmosphere. The squadron leader will establish the regular procedure of the camp. Once they have disposed of their knapsacks, the leader will choose the suitable site for camping. He must select a site which overlooks the zone, providing for two or three ways to escape. He will choose among his men and give them responsibilities such as:

- Cleaning the camp area.

- Adequate drainage in case of rain. Also build trenches or holes for shooting in case of emergency. Likewise he will build the kitchen, which will be built by making a few small ditches and placing three rocks on them; in case the kitchen is built on a pedestal, it will be filled with clay and rocks.

- Build a wall for protection against the wind, the top and sides of which will be covered with branches and leaves of the same vegetation that is present in the zone. This will serve as camouflage and protection from being seen from the air or by enemy patrols in the surrounding areas.

- Build a latrine and dig a hole where all wastes and trash will be buried; these must be covered with earth when the camp is abandoned.

- Once the camp has been established, we recommend the establishment of a watch post at access points and at a reasonable distance, from where a cry of alarm could be heard. At that same time, a password, which must be changed every 14 hours, will be established. The commander must have previously established an alternate meeting point, in case the camp has to be abandoned suddenly, so that they can meet at this other previously established point. The patrol must be warned that if they cannot come together at the established point in a certain amount of time, they must have a third meeting point.

These procedures contribute to the guerrilla's motivation and improve the spirit of cooperation within the unit. The danger, the insecurity, the anxiety and the daily anxiety [entailed] in the life of a guerrilla establish the need for tangible evidence of belonging in order [for the soldiers] to retain their good spirits and morale.

In addition to good physical condition, the guerrilla must be in good physical condition. [To achieve this], we recommend group discussions and self-criticism, which will greatly benefit the spirit and morale of the guerrillas.

Striking camp with the effort and cooperation of all strengthens their esprit de corps. The guerrilla will then be inclined towards a unity of thought in their democratic objectives.

5. <u>Interaction with the People</u>

To ensure popular support, which is essential to the good development of guerrilla warfare, the leaders must lead to positive interaction between civilians and guerrillas, by the principle of "live, eat and work with the people", and they should maintain control of this activity. In group discussions, the leaders and political cadres must emphasize a positive identification with the people.

Talking about tactical military plans in discussions with civilians is not recommended. The communist enemy must be identified as the number one enemy of the people, and as a secondary threat against our guerrilla forces.

As long as there is an opportunity, we must choose groups of elements who have a high degree of political awareness and high discipline in the work to be performed, to be sent to populated areas in order to conduct the armed propaganda. They must persuade people through dialogue in face-to-face encounters, following these principles:

- Respect of human rights and respect of the other's property.
- Helping people in community work.
- Protecting people from communist aggression.
- Teaching environmental hygiene or reading to the people, etc., in order to win their trust, which will result in a better ideological democratic preparation.

These activities will arouse the peasant's sympathy towards our movement, and he will immediately become one of ours, through logistical support, cover and intelligence information about the enemy, or participation in combat. Guerrillas must be persuasive through the word, and not overbearing through their weapons. When they behave this way, the people will feel that they are respected, and will be more inclined to accept our message, thus consolidating popular support.

Any place where tactical guerrilla operations are conducted in highly populated areas, the squadron must also carry out parallel psychological actions, which must precede, accompany and consolidate the common objective, and give explanations to all people about our struggle, indicating that our presence means to give peace, liberty and democracy to all Nicaraguans without exception, and explaining that our struggle is not against the nationals, but rather against Russian imperialism. This will serve to assure greater psychological achievements to augment the tactical operations of the future.

6. <u>Conclusions</u>

The nature of the guerrilla warfare environment does not permit sophisticated facilities for psychological operations, and face-to-face persuasion from the propagandist-combatant guerrillas towards the people is an effective and available tool, which we must use as often as possible during the process of the struggle.

III. ARMED PROPAGANDA

1. General Background

There is frequently a misunderstanding about "armed propaganda", that this tactic consists in prevailing over people with arms. In reality, it does not involve force, but the guerrilla must be very knowledgeable in the principles and methods of this tactic. The objective of this section is to give the guerrilla student an understanding of the armed propaganda that must be used, and which can be applied in guerrilla warfare.

2. Close identification with the People

Armed propaganda includes all actions performed by an armed force, the results of which will bring a better attitude from the people toward that force, not including indoctrination. This is performed by a close identification with the people at any opportunity. For example:

- Hanging up one's arms and working side by side with the peasants in the field: building, fishing, carrying water, fixing roofs, etc.

- When you work with people, the guerrillas can use slogans like: "Many hands doing small things, but doing them together".

- Participating in the people's work you can establish a strong bond between them and the guerrillas, and at the same time, you generate popular support for our movement.

During patrols or other operations near or in the middle of towns, each guerrilla must be respectful and polite with the people. Likewise, he must move cautiously and always be ready to fight, if necessary. But he must not see everyone as an enemy, with suspicion or hostility. Even in war, it is possible to smile, laugh and greet people. Truly, the reason for our revolutionary base, the reason why we fight, is our people. We must be respectful towards them at all times.

In place and situations whenever it's possible, for example, while resting during a march, the guerrillas can explain to youths and children how to handle arms. They can give them an unloaded rifle, so that they can learn to assemble it and disassemble it, how to use it; and they can point to imaginary target, since they are potential recruits for our forces.

The guerrillas must always be ready with easy slogans, to explain to the people, whether by chance or intentionally, the reason for using arms.

- "Arms will be used to win freedom, they are for you".

- "With arms we can set demands, such as hospitals, schools, better roads and social services for the people, for you".

- "Our arms are, truly, the arms of the people, your arms".

- "With arms we can change the Sandinista-communist regime and return to the people a true democracy, so that we all may have economic opportunities".

All of this must be designed to create an identification of the people with arms and with the guerrillas who carry them. Lastly, we must make the people feel that we are thinking about them, and that the arms belong to the people, to help them and to protect them from a communist, totalitarian, imperialist regime, which is indifferent to the needs of the population.

3. Implicit and Explicit Terror

An armed guerrilla force always entails an implicit terror, because the population, without saying it aloud, is afraid that the arms could be used against them. However, if the terror is not made to be explicit, positive results can be expected.

In a revolution, the individual lives under a constant threat of physical harm. If the government police cannot put a halt to guerrilla activities, the population will lose confidence in the government, which has the inherent mission of guaranteeing public safety. However, the guerrillas must be careful not to become an explicit terror, because this would result in a loss of public support.

In the words of a leader of the HUK guerrilla movement[17], in the Philippines:

> The population is always impressed by arms, but not because of the fear that they cause, but rather because they give a feeling of strength. We must present ourselves before the people, supporting them with our arms, and this will give them the message of the struggle.

This is, in a few words, the essence of armed propaganda. An armed guerrilla force may occupy an entire town or small city that is neutral or relatively passive with regard to the conflict. In order to carry out armed propaganda effectively, the following must be done simultaneously:

- Destroy military or police installations, and moving the survivors to a "public place".
- Cut all external lines of communication: cables, radio,

---

17 HUK stands for Hukbong Bayan Laban sa Hapo. It was a Philippines-based Marxist-Leninist guerrilla movement active from 1940s to 1950s.

messengers.

- Set up ambushes, in order to delay efforts on all possible access routes.

- Kidnap all Sandinista government officials and agents, and replacing them in "public places" by military or civil personnel trusted by our movement; in addition do the following:

  - Establish a public court dependent on the guerrillas, and going through the entire town or city, gathering the population together for this act.

  - Shame, ridicule and humiliate the "personal symbols" of the repressive government in the presence of the people, and promoting popular participation by means of guerrillas placed within the crowd, yelling slogans and taunts.

  - Reduce the influence of individuals sympathetic to the regime, exposing their weaknesses and removing them from the town, without damaging them publicly.

  - Mix the guerrillas into the population, and have all members of the column demonstrate very good conduct, practicing the following:

    - Any article taken will be paid for in cash.

    - The hospitality offered by the people will be accepted and this opportunity will be exploited to carry out face-to-face persuasion regarding the struggle.

– Courtesy calls must be paid to prominent and prestigious citizens of the place, such as doctors, priests, teachers, etc.

– The guerrillas must instruct the population, so that when the operation is over and the repressive Sandinista forces interrogate them, they may reveal EVERYTHING about the military operation carried out. For example, the kinds of weapons used, how many men arrived, from what direction they arrived and in what direction they left, in other words, EVERYTHING.

– Likewise, indicate to the population that in meetings or in private discussions, they may give the names of Sandinista informers, who will be removed together with the other officials of the repressive government.

– When conducting a meeting, conclude it with a speech by one of the guerrilla leaders or political cadres (the most dynamic one), including explicit references to:

  – The fact that the "enemies of the people", the Sandinista officials or agents, must not be mistreated in spite of the criminal actions, even though the guerrilla forces may have suffered casualties, and that this is done thanks to the generosity of the Christian guerrillas.

- Give a statement of thanks for the "hospitality" of the population, as well as let them know that the risks that they will run when the Sandinista return are greatly appreciated.

- The fact that the Sandinista regime will not be able to resist the attacks of our guerrilla forces, in spite of the fact that they exploit the people with taxes, control of currency, grain, and all aspects of public life through the associations, to which they are forced to belong.

- Making a promise to the people that they will return to make sure that the "leeches" of the repressive Sandinista regime will not be able to impede the integration of our guerrilla with the population.

- A repeated statement to the population to the effect that they may reveal everything about this visit by our commandos, because we are not afraid of anything or anyone, or either the Soviets or the Cubans. Emphasize that we are

Nicaraguans, that we struggle for Nicaragua's freedom, and to establish a wholly Nicaraguan government.

4. Guerrilla Arms are the Strength of the People Against an Illegal Government

Armed propaganda in populated areas does not give the impression that the arms are the power of the guerrillas over the people, but rather that the arms are the strength of the people against a repressive regime. Whenever it is necessary to use armed force during an occupation or a visit to a town or village, the guerrillas must emphasize and make sure during this action that they:

- Explain to the population that first of all this is being done to protect them, the people, not the guerrillas themselves.

- Admit frankly and publicly that this is "an act of democratic guerrilla", with the appropriate explanations.

- That this action, although not desirable, is necessary because the final objective of the insurrection is a free and democratic society, where acts of force are not necessary.

- The force of arms is a need provoked by the oppressive system, and will cease to exist when the "forces of justice" of our movement assume control.

- If, for example, it became necessary for one of the advance posts to have to shoot a citizen who was trying to leave the town or city in which the guerrillas are carrying out armed propaganda or political proselytism, the following is recommended:

  - Explain that if this citizen were able to escape, he would avert the enemy near the town or city, and they would come in with reprisals such as rape, pillage, destruction, captures, etc., terrorizing the inhabitants of the place for having been attentive and hospitable to the guerrillas in the town.

  - <u>If a guerrilla shoots an individual, make the population see that he was an enemy of the people, and that they shot him because the guerrilla recognized their primordial duty, which is protecting the citizens.</u>

  - The commando tried to stop the informant without shooting, because he, like all Christian guerrillas, advocate non-violence. Having shot the Sandinista informer, although is against his own will, was necessary to avoid repression on the part of the Sandinista government against the innocent people.

  - Make the population see that it was the regime's repressive system, which caused this situation, that really killed the informant, and that the weapon fired was one that was recovered in combat against the Sandinista regime.

- Make the population see that if the Sandinista regime had ended its repression, with the corruption sponsored by foreign powers, etc., the freedom commandos would not have had to take up arms to cut down the lives of their Nicaraguan brothers, which hurts our Christian feelings. If the informant had not tried to escape, he would be enjoying life together with the rest of the population, because he would not have tried to inform to the enemy. This death would have been avoided if justice and freedom existed in Nicaragua, and this is exactly the objective of the democratic guerrilla.

5. <u>Selective Use of Violence for Propaganda Effects</u>

We could <u>neutralize</u> carefully selected and planned-for targets, such as court judges, cattle judges (*jueces de mesta*), police or state security officers, CDS chiefs[18], etc. For purposes of the psychological effect, it is necessary to take extreme precautions, and it is essential to gather the affected population together to attend, take part in the act, and formulate accusations

---

18 CDS is acronym for Comités de Defensa Sandinista, which means Sandinista Defense Committees.

against the oppressor.

The target or person must be selected on the basis of the following:

- The spontaneous hostility which the majority of the population may feel against the target.
- Using potential rejection or hate on the part of the majority of the affected population against the target, rousing the population and making them see all of the individual's negative and hostile act against the people.
- If the majority of the people supports or backs the target, don't try to change these feelings through provocation.

In relation to the difficulty of handling the person who will replace the target, the person who will replace the target must be selected carefully, on the basis of the following:

- Degree of violence necessary to effect the change.
- Degree of violence acceptable to the affected population.
- Degree of violence possible without causing damage or danger to other individuals in the area around the target.
- Foreseeable degree of reprisals on the part of the enemy towards the affected population or other individuals in the area around the target.

The mission of replacing the individual must be followed by:

- Extensive explanations to the affected population of why [this action] was necessary for the good of the people.

- Explaining that the Sandinista reprisals are unfair, indiscriminate, and above all, a justification for the execution of this mission.

- Carefully sounding out the reaction of the people to the mission, as well as controlling this reaction by assuring that the population's reaction is beneficial to the Freedom Commandos.

6. <u>Conclusions</u>

Armed propaganda includes all actions performed and the impact achieved by an armed force, resulting in positive attitudes on the part of the population towards that force, not including forced indoctrination. However, armed propaganda is the most effective instrument available to a guerrilla force.

IV. ARMED PROPAGANDA TEAMS

1. <u>General</u>

In contact with the very reality of their roots, in a campaign of psychological operations in guerrilla warfare, the commanders will be able to obtain maximum psychological results from a program of Armed Propaganda Teams. The purpose of this section is to inform the student guerrilla of what the Armed Propaganda Teams are in the milieu of guerrilla warfare.

2. <u>Combination: Political Awareness and Armed Propaganda</u>

The Armed Propaganda Teams combine political consciousness raising with armed propaganda, which will be conducted by carefully selected guerrilla (preferably with combat experience), for personal persuasion within the population.

The selection of personnel is more important than the training, because we cannot train guerrilla cadres solely to demonstrate the feelings of ardor and fervor, which are essential since person-to-person persuasion is important. However, it is even more important to train persons who are intellectually cultivated and agile.

An Armed Propaganda Team includes from 6 to 10 members. This number, or a smaller number, is ideal, because then there is more camaraderie, solidarity, and esprit de corps. The subject discussed are assimilated more readily, and the members react more rapidly to unexpected situations.

In addition to being a combined armed combatant and propagandist, each member of the team must be well prepared to conduct constant person-to-person, face-to-face communications.

The leader of the team will have to be the commander who is most highly motivated politically and most effective in face-to-face persuasion. Position, hierarchy, or rank will not be the determining factor for performing this function, but rather it will be performed by whoever is best qualified for communication with the people.

The source of basic recruitment for guerrilla cadres will be the same social groups of Nicaraguans toward whom the psychological campaign is directed, such as peasants, students, professionals, housewives, etc. The peasants must be made to see that they have no land; the workers, that the state is closing down the factories and industries; the doctor, that they are being displaced by Cuban paramedics, and that as doctors they cannot exercise their profession because of lack of drugs. A requirement for recruiting them will be their skill in expressing themselves in public.

The selection of personnel is more important than the training. Individual consciousness raising and capacity of persuasion in the discussions of groups for motivation of the guerrilla as combatant-propagandist, selecting as cadres and organizing into teams those who have the greatest capacity for this work.

The training of guerrillas for armed propaganda teams is focused on the method, not on the content. A training of two weeks is sufficient if the recruitment is conducted in the form indicated. If a wrong selection process has been followed, the individual selected will not produce a very good result, no matter how good the training provided.

The training will have to be intensive for 14 days, by means of discussions within the team, alternating the position of discussion leader among the members of the group.

The topics to be discussed will be the same; a different

topic will be introduced each day, for varied practice.

The topics will have to refer to the local conditions and to the significance which they have for the residents of the locality, such as speaking about crops, fertilizers, seeds, irrigation, etc. The following topics may also be included:

- Lumber, tiles, carpentry tools for houses and other buildings;
- Boats, launches, roads, horses, oxen for transportation, fishing, and agriculture;
- Problems which they may have locally with neighbors, offices of the regime, visitors, taxes, etc.;
- Forced labor, service in the militias;
- Forced association in Sandinista groupings, such as women's clubs, youth associations, workers associations, etc.;
- Availability and prices of consumer goods and articles of prime necessity in local grocery stores and shops;
- Characteristics of the education in public schools;
- Concern of the population about the presence of Cuban teachers in the schools and political interference, that is, using the schools for political purposes rather than for educational purposes, as they should be used;
- Indignation over the lack of freedom of religion and over

the persecution of which the priests are victims; and over the participation of priests such as D'Escoto and Cardenal in the Sandinista government, against the explicit orders of His Holiness the Pope.

Note: Other topics may be developed by the members of the team.

The target groups for the Armed Propaganda Teams are not the persons with sophisticated political knowledge but those whose opinions are formed from what they see and hear. The cadres will have to use persuasion to carry out their mission. Some of the methods of persuasion which may be used are the following:

- Internal group/external group. It is a principle of psychology that we humans have a tendency to make personal associations of "we" and "the others" or "we" and "they"; "friends" and "enemies"; "compatriots" and "foreigners"; "Latinos" and "gringos".

- The Armed Propaganda Teams can use this principle in its activities so that it may be obvious that the "external" groups ("false" groups) are those of the Sandinista regime, and that the "internal" groups ("true" groups) which fight for the people are the Freedom Commandos.

– We must inculcate this in the people in a subtle manner, so that these sentiments may seem to be born of themselves, spontaneously.

– "Against" is easier than "for". It is a principle of political sciences that it is easier to persuade the people to vote against something or someone than to persuade them to vote in favor of something or someone. Although at present the regime has not given the Nicaraguan people the opportunity to vote, it is known that the people will vote against it, for which reason the Armed Propaganda Teams can use this principle in favor of our insurrectional struggle. They will have to make sure that this campaign is directed specifically against the government or its sympathizers, since the people must have specific targets for their frustrations.

– Primary groups and secondary groups. Another principle of sociology is that we humans form or change our opinions from two sources: primarily, through our association with our relatives, work colleagues, or intimate friends; and secondarily, through distant associations such as acquaintances in churches, clubs, or committees, or labor unions and government organizations. The cadres of Armed Propaganda Teams will have to associate themselves with the primary groups, for the purpose of persuading them to follow the policy of our movement, because it is from this type of groups that opinions or changes of opinions come.

Techniques of Persuasion in Chats and Speeches

- Be simple and concise. Avoid the use of difficult words or expressions. Prefer popular words and expressions, that is, the language of the people. In dealing with a person, make use of concise language, avoiding complicated verbiage. It should be recalled that we use oratory to make our people understand the reason for our struggle and not to show our knowledge.

- Use vivid and realistic examples. Avoid abstract concepts, such as those used in universities in the higher years; instead of them, give concrete examples such as children playing, horses galloping, birds in flight, etc.

- Use gestures to communicate. In addition to verbal communication, we can communicate through gestures, such as moving our hands expressively, movements of the back, facial expressions, focusing our glance, and other aspects of "body language", projecting the individual personality in the message.

- Use the appropriate tone of voice. If in addressing the

people one speaks about happiness, one will have to use a
happy tone. If one speaks of something sad, the tone of
voice must be of sadness; in speaking of a heroic act or act
of valor, one will speak with an animated voice, etc.

- Above all, be natural. One must avoid imitating others,
since people, especially simple people, can easily detect a
charlatan. One will have to project one's individual
personality when addressing the population.

3. **<u>"Eyes and Ears" within the Population</u>**

The abundance of information for intelligence which the
deployment of Armed Propaganda Teams will generate will
permit us to cover a large area with our commandos, who will
become the eyes and ears of our movement within the population.

- The combined reports of an Armed Propaganda Team
program will provide us with details on enemy activities.

- The intelligence information obtained by the Armed
Propaganda Team cadres will have to be reported to the
chiefs. Nevertheless, it is necessary to emphasize that the
first mission of the Armed Propaganda Teams is to
conduct psychological operations, not to obtain
intelligence information. Any intelligence report will be
made through external contact of the Armed Propaganda

Team, so as not to compromise the population.

- The Armed Propaganda cadres are capable of doing what others cannot do in a guerrilla campaign: determine personally the development of deterioration of popular support, and the sympathy or hostility which the people feel toward our movement.

- The program of Armed Propaganda Teams, in addition to being very effective psychologically, increases the capacity of the guerrilla group to obtain and use the information.

- Likewise, the Armed Propaganda Cadre will report to his superior the reaction of the people to the radio broadcasts, insurrectional leaflets, or any other medium of our propaganda.

- The expression or gestures of the eyes and face, the tone and strength of the voice, and the use of suitable words greatly influence face-to-face persuasion with the people.

With the intelligence reports supplied by the Armed Propaganda Teams, the commanders will have exact knowledge of the popular support, which they will use in their operations.

4. **<u>Psychological Tactics, Maximum Flexibility</u>**

Psychological tactics will have the maximum flexibility within a general plan, permitting a continuous and immediate adjustment of the message, and making sure to create an impact on the indicated target group, at the moment at which it is most susceptible.

Tactically, a program of Armed Propaganda Teams should cover the greater part, and, if possible, all of the operational territory. The communities in which the propaganda will be conducted will not necessarily have to coincide with political units of an official character. A complete understanding of their structure or organization is not necessary, because the cadres will operate by applying social-political action and not academic theory.

The target populations of the Armed Propaganda Teams will be selected because they are part of the operational area, and not because of their size or the extent of their territory.

- The objective will have to be the people, not the territorial area.

- In this respect, each work team will have to cover approximately six population centers, for the purpose of developing popular support for our movement. The team will always have to move in a covert manner within the population centers of its area. It will have to vary its route radically, but not its itinerary. This is so that the inhabitants who are cooperating may depend on its itinerary, that is, on the time at which they may frequently contact it to give it information.

– The danger of betrayal or ambush can be neutralized by varying the itinerary slightly, using different routes, as well as by arriving or leaving without advance noticed:

  – While the surprise factor is used, vigilance will have to be exercised in order to detect the possible presence of hostile elements.

  – One should not stay more than three consecutive days in one populated place.

  – The three-day limit has obvious tactical advantages, but it also creates a psychological effect on the people when they see the team as a source of current and up-to-date information. Also, it may overexpose the target audience and cause a negative reaction.

Basic tactical precautions will have to be taken. This is necessary for greater effectiveness, as was indicated in the discussion of the topic of "Armed Propaganda". When it is conducted in a discreet manner, it increases the respect of the population for the team and enhances its credibility.

The basic procedures are: covert elements who exercise vigilance before and after the departure and at intervals. There should be at least two of them, and they should meet at a predetermined place at a signal or before any hostile action.

The goal of the team is to motivate the entire population of a place, but to remain constantly aware that specific target groups exist within this general configuration of the public.

Although meetings are held in the populated place, the cadres will have to recognize, and keep in contact with, the target groups, mingling with them before, during, and after the meeting. The method of conducting this type of meeting was included in the topic of "Armed Propaganda", and it will be covered in greater detail under the title of "Control of Mass Meetings and Demonstrations".

The primary focus of the Armed Propaganda cadres will have to be on the residents of the populated place, where their knowledge as shapers of opinion can be applied.

On the first visits of identification with the inhabitants, the guerrilla cadres will be polite and humble. They can work in the fields or in any other way in which their skills can contribute to improving the standard of living of the local inhabitants, winning their confidence and talking with them; helping them to repair the fences of their pastures and to clean them; helping them in vaccinating their animals; teaching them to read – that is, living closely together with them in all tasks characteristic of the peasant or the community.

In their free time, our guerrillas should mingle with the community groups and participate with them in community activities, fiestas, birthdays, and even in wakes or burials of members of the community. They will try to talk with both adults and adolescents. They will try to penetrate within the family, in order to gain the acceptance and trust of all the residents of the sector.

The cadres of the Armed Propaganda Teams will give ideological training, mixing these instructions with folk songs, and at the same time telling stories which have some attraction, trying to have them allude to heroic acts of our ancestors. They will also try to tell of the acts of heroism of our fighters in the present struggle, so that the listeners may try to imitate them. It is important to let them know that there are other countries in the world, where freedom and democracy cause the rulers to concern themselves with the welfare of their people, in order that the children have medical attention and free education; where they also concern themselves with seeing that everyone has job and food and all freedoms, such as those of religion, association, and expression; where the greatest objective of the government is to keep its people happy.

The cadres should mention their political ideology during

the first phase of identifying with the people and talks should be oriented towards subjects which are pleasant for the peasants or those who are listening trying to be as plain as possible to be well understood.

The tactical objectives for identification with the people are the following:

- Establishing close relations through an identification with the people, by means of the same customs.

- Determining the basic needs and desires of the different target groups.

- Discovering the weaknesses of the government control.

- Little by little, sowing the seed of democratic revolution, in order to change the vices of the regime towards a new order of justice and collective well-being.

- In the motivation of the target groups by the Armed Propaganda Teams, the cadre must apply themes of "true" and "false" groups. The true group will be the target group and the false will be the Sandinista regime.

- Before the economic interest groups, such as small businessmen and farmers, we must emphasize that their potential advantages are "limited" by the Sandinista government, that the resources are increasingly scarce, profits are minimum, taxes high, etc. This may be applied to transportation entrepreneurs and others.

- For elements ambitious for power and social position, we will emphasize that they will never be able to belong to the government social class, since their circles of power are hermetically closed. For example, the nine Sandinista leaders do not allow other people to participate in the government, and they impede the development of the economic and social potential of those who, like them, have the desire to better themselves, which is unfair and arbitrary.

- Social and intellectual criticism. They must be channeled towards the professionals, professors, teachers, priests, missionaries, students and others. They must see that their writings, comments or conversations are censored, which does not allow a correction of these problems.

Once the needs and frustrations of the target groups have been determined, the hostility of the people toward the "false" groups will become more direct against the present regime and its repressive system. The people will be made to see that once this system or structure is eliminated, the cause of their frustrations would be eliminated and they could make their wishes come true. It must become evident for the population that supporting the insurrection is really supporting their own desires, since the democratic movement is aimed at the elimination of these specific problems.

As a general rule, the Armed Propaganda Teams should avoid participating in combat. However, if this is not possible, they must react as a guerrilla unit with "hit-and-run" activities, inflicting the greatest amount of casualties on the enemy with aggressive assault fire, recovering enemy weapons and withdrawing quickly.

An exception to the rule of avoiding combat shall be when they are challenged in the town by hostile actions, be it by an individual or by an equal number of men from the enemy side.

Hostility from one or two men can be dominated by eliminating the enemy in a quick and efficient manner. This is the most common danger.

When the enemy is equal in numbers, they must withdraw immediately, and later ambush them, or eliminate them by means of sharpshooters.

In any case, the cadres from the Armed Propaganda Teams must not turn the town into a battlefield. Usually, our guerrillas will be better armed, for which reason they will obtain greater respect from the population if they carry out opportune maneuvers instead of putting their lives in anger, or even destroying their homes in an encounter with the enemy inside the town.

5. <u>A Tight-Knit Program of Teams: Mobile Infrastructure</u>

The psychological operations carried out through the Armed Propaganda Teams include the infiltration of key guerrilla communicators (i.e., cadres of Armed Propaganda Teams) among the country's populace instead of sending messages to them through outside sources, thus creating our "mobile infrastructure".

A "mobile infrastructure" is a cadre from our armed propaganda team moving around, i.e., maintaining contact among six or more towns, from where their source of information will come; and at the same time it will be used so that at an opportune time they can be integrated into the full guerrilla movement.

In this way, a program of Armed Propaganda Teams in the operational area builds for our commanders in the field a source for the continual gathering and compiling of data (infrastructure) on the entire area. It is also a means to develop and increase popular support, to recruit new members, and to obtain supplies.

In the same way, a program of Armed Propaganda Teams allows the expansion of the guerrilla movement since these teams can penetrate areas which are not under the control of the combat units. In this way, through an exact evaluation of the combat units they will be able to plan their operations more precisely since they will have a sure knowledge of the existing conditions.

The commanders will remember that these types of

operations, such as the Fifth Column, were used in the first part of the Second World War and that using infiltration and subversion tactics allowed the Germans to penetrate the target countries before the invasions. They succeeded in entering Poland, Belgium, Holland and France in a month; Norway in a week. The effectiveness of this tactic has been clearly demonstrated in several wars, and it can be used effectively by Commandos of Freedom.

The activities of the Armed Propaganda Teams run some risk, but no greater than any other guerrilla activity. Nevertheless, the Armed Propaganda Teams are essential for the success of the struggle.

6. <u>Conclusions</u>

The same way in which scouts are the "eyes and ears" of a patrol, or of a column on the march, the Armed Propaganda Teams are also the source of information, the "antennas" of our movement because they find and exploit the socio-political weaknesses in the target society, making possible a good operation.

V. DEVELOPMENT AND CONTROL OF FRONT ORGANIZATIONS

1. <u>Generalities</u>

The development and control of front organizations (or "facade" organizations) is an essential process in the guerrilla effort to realize the insurrection. This is actually an aspect of urban guerrilla wars, but it must advance parallel to the campaign in the countryside.

The objective of this section is to give the guerrilla student an understanding about the development and control of front organizations in guerrilla warfare.

2. <u>Initial Recruitment</u>

The initial recruitment to the movement if involuntary will be carried out by means of several "private" consultations with a cadre (without the recruit realizing that he is speaking to one of our members). Afterwards, the recruit will be informed that he or she is already in the movement, and will be running the risk of [being caught by the] government police if he or she does not cooperate.

When the guerrillas carry out missions of armed

propaganda and a program of regular visits to the towns by Armed Propaganda Teams, these contacts will provide to the commanders the names and places of persons that can be recruited. Voluntary recruitment is effected by means of visits from guerrilla leaders or political cadres.

After a chain of voluntary recruitments has been developed, and their reliability has been established by completing some minor missions, they will be instructed on widening the chain by recruiting in specific target groups, according to the following procedure:

- From among their acquaintances or through observation of the target groups—political parties, labor unions, youth groups, farming organizations, etc.—find out the personal habits, preferences and aversions, as well as the weaknesses of the "recruitable" individuals.

- Make an approach through an acquaintance, and, if possible, develop a friendship, attracting (the individual) by means of his preferences or weaknesses; possibly by inviting him to lunch in a restaurant he likes, or to have a drink in his favorite bar, or an invitation to dinner in a place he prefers.

Recruitment should follow one of the following patterns:

- If in an informal conversation the target seems susceptible to voluntary recruitment based on his beliefs and personal values, etc., the political cadre assigned to carry out recruitments will be notified. The original contact will indicate to the assigned cadre in detail all that he knows about the possible recruit, and the style of persuasion that should be used, and introduce the two.

- If the target does not seem susceptible to voluntary recruitment, meetings which will seem accidental can be arranged with guerrilla leaders of political cadre (unknown to the target until then). The meeting will be done so that "other persons" know that the target was there, because they saw him arrive at a certain house, or seated at a table in a certain bar, or even seated on a park bench. The target is then confronted with the fact of his participation in the insurrection and he will also be told that if he fails to cooperate or to carry out future orders, he will expose himself to reprisals on the part of the regime's police or military.

- Notification of the police, informing on a target who refuses to join the guerrillas, can be easily carried out, when it is necessary, by means of a letter with false declarations by citizens who are not implicated in the movement. Care must be taken so that the person who recruited him covertly should not be uncovered.

– With the completion of clandestine missions for the movement, the involvement and commitment of each recruit will gradually become greater, and his confidence will increase. This should be a gradual process, in order to prevent confessions from frightened individuals to whom very difficult or dangerous missions have been assigned too early.

Using this recruiting techniques, our guerrilla can successfully infiltrate any key target group in the regime, in order to improve internal control over the enemy structure.

3. Established Citizens, Subjective Control

Established citizens—such as doctors, lawyers, businessmen, landowners, minor state officials, etc.—will be recruited into the movement and used for the subjective internal control of groups and associations to which they belong or may belong.

Once the recruitment/involvement has been accomplished, and has progressed to a point of reliability which permits specific instructions to be given to the cadre in order to begin to influence their groups, directions will be given to them to carry out the following:

- The procedure is simple and requires only a basic knowledge of Socratic dialectics: that is the knowledge which is inherent to another person or to the established position of a group; some topic, come word or thought related to the goal of persuasion of our person in charge of recruitment.

- The member then should introduce this topic, work or thought into the discussions or meetings of the target group, by means of a casual remark, which will improve the focus of other group members in relation to it (the topic, etc.). Specific examples are:

  - Groups of economic interests are motivated by profit, and generally feel that the system prevents the use of their abilities in this effort in some way, taxes, import/export tariffs, transportation costs, etc. The cadre in charge (of recruitment) will make this feeling of frustration increase in later conversations.

  - Political aspirants, especially if they are not successful, feel that the system discriminates against them unjustly by limiting their capabilities, because the Sandinista regime does not permit elections. The cadre should channel political discussions towards this frustration.

- Social and intellectual critics (such as professors, teachers, priests, missionaries, etc.) generally feel that the government ignores their valid criticisms and unjustly censors their commentaries, especially in a revolutionary situation. This can be easily demonstrated by the guerrilla member as an injustice of the system, in meetings and discussions.

- In all of the target groups, after the frustrations have been established, the hostility towards the obstacles to their aspirations will gradually be transferred toward the present regime and its system of repression.

The guerrilla cadre working among the target groups should always maintain a low-key presence, so that the development of hostile feelings towards the Sandinista regime will seem to come spontaneously from the group's members, and not from the cadre's suggestions. This is subjective internal control.

The anti-government hostility should be generalized and not necessarily in our favor.

If a group develops a favorable feeling towards us it can be used. But the main goal is to prearrange the target groups to be included latter in the mass organizations for the operation when some other activities have been developed successfully.

4. <u>Organization of Cells for Security</u>

Internal cadres of our movement should be organized into cells of three persons, with only one of them having contact outside of the cell.

The three-man cell is the basic element of the movement; it has frequent meetings in order to receive orders and pass on information to the cell leader. These meetings are also very important for the cell members' encouragement of each other as well as for their morale. They should carry out self-criticism on the successes and failures in completing individual missions of subjective control.

Coordination of the three-member cell provides a secure network for two-way communication, each member having contact with only one operational cell. Members shall not reveal in cell coordination meetings the identity of their contact in an operational cell; they shall divulge only the nature of the activity in which the cell is involved, e.g., political party work, medical association work.

There is no hierarchy of cells beyond an element of coordination with the Zone Commanders through whom direct, but secret, contact will be maintained with the commander of our guerrilla group in the operational area or zone. The diagram that follows (see "Cell Organization Diagram), in Additional Material) does not indicate which new operational cell is the limit, but indicates that for every three operational cells we need a coordination cell.

5. <u>Incorporation into a "Front" Organization</u>

The merging of organizations recognized by the Sandinist government, such as associations and other groups, through internal subjective control occurs in the final stages of the operation, in close relationship with mass meetings.

When armed guerrilla action has spread sufficiently, large-scale armed propaganda missions will be conducted: propaganda teams will have clearly expressed open support for the institutions; the enemy system of target groups will be well infiltrated; and the preparation of these groups when mass meetings are held. The internal cadres will have to start discussions toward the "merging" of forces into an organization—this organization shall be a front "facade" group of our movement.

Any other target group will be aware that other groups are evincing a greater hostility toward the government, the police, and the traditional legal bases of authority. The guerrilla cadres in that group, such as teachers, will cultivate this awareness by making comments like "so and so, who is a farmer, said that members of his cooperative believe that the new economic policy is absurd, poorly planned and unfair to the farmers".

When awareness that other groups are hostile to the regime is increased, group discussions are held openly and our movement will be able to receive reports that most of its operations are equally shared. There will develop greater hostility toward the regime and the order to merge will come forth. The incorporation into a "facade" organization is undertaken as follows:

- Internal (cadres) from our movement will meet with others in positions of leadership, such as presidents, leaders, and others, in organized meetings presided by the organization's chief of our movement. Two or three escorts may assist the guerrilla cadre if it becomes necessary.
- Following the meeting a joint communique is to be issued, announcing the creation of the "facade" organization, including names and signatures of participants and names of the organizations they represent.
- Following the issuance of this communique, mass meetings should be initiated, whose aim must be the destruction of the Sandinist control system.

6. <u>Conclusions</u>

The development and control of "facade" organizations in guerrilla warfare will provide our movement with the capability of creating the effect of a "backlash" within the population when the order to merge is given.

When infiltration and internal subjective control have been developed alongside other guerrilla activities, one commander of the democratic guerrilla could literally shake up and replace the Sandinist structure.

VI. CONTROL OF THE MASSES AND MEETINGS

1. <u>Generalities</u>

During the last stages of a guerrilla struggle; meetings and mass concentrations are a powerful psychological instrument to carry out the mission.

The purpose of this section is to train the guerrilla student on techniques on meetings and mass concentrations in guerrilla warfare.

2. <u>Infiltration of Guerrilla Cadres</u>

- Infiltration of guerrilla cadres (either a member of our own movement or an outside member) in trade unions, youth movements, peasant organizations, etc., preconditioning these groups to act among the masses, where they will have to proselytize in a clandestine fashion for the insurrectional struggle.

- Our psychological war team must develop in advance a hostile mental attitude among the target groups, so that at the given moment they can turn their anger into violence, demanding their rights taken away by the regime.

- These preconditioning campaigns will be aimed at the

political parties, professional organizations, students, workers, the unemployed masses, the ethnic minorities, and at any other vulnerable or recruitable sector of society; this also includes the popular masses and sympathizers to our movement.

- The principal objective of a preconditioning campaign is to create a negative "image" of the common enemy, for example:

  - To describe managers of government collective entities as "slave drivers" in their treatment of the personnel.

  - To say that the police mistreat the people the same as the communist "gestapo".

  - To say that the officials of the Government of National Reconstruction are lackeys of Cuban-Soviet imperialism.

- Our psychological warfare cadres will create temporary compulsive obsessions in mass concentrations or group meetings by hammering on specific or selective topics; in informal conversations by expressing discontent; writing editorials for newspapers and radio, aimed at conditioning the people's thinking for the decisive moment, at which time they will turn to general violence.

- To facilitate the preconditioning of the masses we must

repeat phrases frequently to let the people know, for instance, that:

– The taxes they pay to the government do not benefit the people at all, and that, on the contrary, they are used in the form of exploitation and to enrich government officials.

– Make evident to them that the people have been turned into slaves, and are being exploited by privileged political and military groups.

– That foreign advisors and their advisory programs are in actuality "interventionists" in our country, that they direct the exploitation of the nation in accordance with the objectives of the Soviet and Cuban imperialists so as to turn our people into slaves of the hammer and sickle.

3. <u>Selection of Appropriate Slogans</u>

The commanders of the guerrilla war select their slogans according to the circumstances, for the purpose of mobilizing the masses in a broad range of activities, and on the highest emotional level.

When the insurrection of the masses is being carried out, our covert cadres should make partial demands, initially demanding for example: "we want food", "we want religious freedom", "we want labor union freedom", steps that will carry us toward the realization of the goals of our movement which are: GOD, COUNTRY AND DEMOCRACY.

If a lack of organization and command is observed in the enemy authority, and the people are in an excited state, this situation may be exploited so that our agitators may raise the tone of the watchword slogans to the point of carrying them to the highest pitch.

If the masses are not emotionally excited, our agitators will continue with the "partial" slogans, and the demands will be based on daily needs, connecting them with the goals of our movement.

An example of the necessity for giving simple slogans is that few people think in terms of millions of Cordobas, but any citizen, however poor he may be, understands that a pair of shoes is a necessity. The goals of the movement are of an ideological nature, but our agitators must keep in mind that food, "bread and butter", "tortilla and heape", win over the people, and they should understand that is their primary mission.

4. <u>Creation of Nuclei</u>

This involves the mobilization of a specific number of

agitators from the guerrilla organization of the village. This group will inevitably attract an equal number of curious individuals who are looking for adventures and thrills, as well as those who are dissatisfied with the system of the government.

The guerrilla will attract sympathizers, citizens who are discontent as a result of the repression [of the government]. To each guerrilla sub-unit will be assigned specific tasks and missions which they should carry out.

Our [cadres] will be mobilized in the largest number possible, together with individuals who have been affected by the communist dictatorship, whether it be that they have been robbed of their possessions, imprisoned, tortured or experienced any other type of aggression against themselves. They will mobilize to the areas where the criminal and hostile members of the FSLN, CDS and others live, making an effort to go armed with clubs, iron bars, placards, and if possible small arms, which they will carry concealed.

If possible, professional criminals will be hired to carry out specific selective "jobs".

Our agitator will visit the villages where unemployed individuals may be present, as well as unemployment offices, in order to hire them for unspecified "jobs". The recruitment of the unsavory individuals is necessary because it creates a nucleus under absolute orders.

The designated cadres will arrange in advance the transportation of the participants so as to take them to the meeting places in private or public vehicles, boats or any other means of transportation.

Other cadres will be designated to make placards, flags and banners with different types of slogans or watchwords, be they of the partial, transitory or of the more radical type.

Other cadres will be designated to prepare leaflets, posters, handbills and pamphlets so as to make the meetings more colorful. This material will contain instructions for the participants, and will also be useful against the regime.

<u>Specific jobs will be assigned to other elements in order to create a "martyr" for the cause, leading the demonstrators into a confrontation with authorities, so as to provoke riots or shootings which may cause the death of one or more persons who would become martyrs, a situation which should be taken advantage of immediately against the regime so as to create greater conflicts.</u>

5. <u>Ways of Carrying Out an Uprising in Mass Meetings</u>

It may be affected by means of a small group of guerrillas infiltrated among the masses, those who will have the mission of agitating, giving the impression that they are numerous and that they have extensive popular support. Employing the tactics of a force of 200 to 300 agitators, a demonstration can be created in which 10,000 to 20,000 persons take part.

Agitation of the masses in a demonstration is carried out by means of socio-political objectives. One or several agents from our covert movement, highly trained as mass agitators, should participate in this action, involving innocent persons so as to provoke an apparently spontaneous protest demonstration. These individuals will direct the entire meeting until its conclusion.

External command. This group stays out of all activities, situated in such a way that it is able to observe the unfolding of the planned events from where it is stationed. As observation point, for example, he should look for a church steeple, a tall building, a tall tree, the highest tier of the stadium or an auditorium, or any other high place.

Internal command. This individual will remain inside the crowd. Great importance should be given to protect the leaders of these individuals. Some placards or allusive banners should be used to designate the Command Posts, and to send signals to the sub-units. This individual will avoid placing himself in locations where fights and incidents could occur after the demonstration begins.

Our key agitators will remain inside the crowd. The person in charge of this mission will in advance instruct the agitators to stay near the placards he has assigned to them, in order to protect the placards from any opponent. This way the commander will know where our agitators are located and will be able to send orders regarding the change of watchwords or slogans or any other unforeseen event, and eventually, if he so desires, he can even encourage violence.

At this stage, one the key cadres are spread out, they should position themselves at visible places, such as signs, light posts, and other conspicuous places.

Our key agitators should avoid places of disturbances, once they have made sure they have started.

Defense Detachment. These individuals will act as moving bodyguards, forming a protective circle around the chief to protect him from the police and the army, or to help him escape if it were necessary. They should be highly disciplined and will only react to a verbal order from the chief.

In the event that the chief takes part in a religious gathering, a funeral, or any other kind of activity which should be conducted in an orderly manner, the bodyguards will remain in the rows that are very close to the chief or to the placard carriers or banners in order to give them the best protection.

The participants in this mission should be guerrilla fighters dressed in civilian clothes, or else hired recruits who sympathize with our struggle and are against the oppressing regime. These members should be very highly disciplined and will use violence only on verbal orders from the person in charge.

Messengers. They should remain close to the leaders, transmitting orders between the external and internal commands. They will make use of radios, telephones, bicycles, motorcycles, automobiles or they will travel on foot or horse, taking trails or paths to shorten the distances. Young adolescent (male and female) are ideal for this type of mission.

Shock troops. These men should be equipped with non-firing weapons (knives, razors, chains, clubs) and should march behind the innocent and unwary participants. They should conceal their weapons. They will take action only as "reinforcement" if the guerrilla agitators are attacked by the police. They will appear in a sudden, violent and surprising manner, in order to distract the authorities, thus making possible the quick retreat or escape of the internal command.

Banners and placards carriers. The banners and placards used in demonstrations or gathering, will express the complaints of the population but when the demonstration arrives to its highest level of euphoria or popular dissatisfaction, our infiltrators will make use of the placards containing slogans and watchwords benefitting our cause and against the regime which we may be able to infiltrate in a covert manner. The person in charge of this mission will in advance instruct the agitators to remain near the placards of any member of the opposition. This way, the commander will know where the agitators are located, and will be able to send orders to change slogans and eventually encourage violence if he so wishes.

Watchword and applause agitators. They will be given specific instructions to use rehearsed watchwords. They will be able to use such phrases as "we are hungry", "we want bread", "we don't want communism".

These tasks and techniques to agitate the masses are quite similar to the ones used by the cheerleaders at high school baseball and football games. The objective is to gain more supporters not just to shout slogans.

6. Conclusions

In a revolutionary movement of guerrilla warfare the gathering of the masses and protest demonstrations are the essential elements for the destruction of the enemy's structure.

VII.   GRASS ROOTS MASSIVE SUPPORT THROUGH PSYOPS

1. <u>Generalities</u>

The separate coverage in these sections could leave the student with some doubts. Therefore, all sections are summarized here, in order to give a clearer picture of this book.

2. <u>Motivation as Combatant-Propagandist</u>

Every member of the struggle should know that his political mission is as important as, if not more important than, his tactical mission.

3. <u>Armed Propaganda</u>

Armed propaganda in small towns, rural villages, and city residential districts should give the impression that our weapons are not for exercising power over the people, but rather that the weapons are for protecting the people; that they are the power of the people against the FSLN[19] government of oppression.

---

19 Frente Sandinista de Liberación Nacional.

4. <u>Armed Propaganda Teams</u>

Armed Propaganda Teams will combine political awareness building and the ability to conduct propaganda for ends of personal persuasion, which will be carried out within the population.

5. <u>Covert ("Facade") Organizations</u>

The fusion of several organizations and associations recognized by the government, through internal subjective control, occurs in the final stages of the operation, in close cooperation with mass meetings.

6. <u>Control of Mass Demonstrations</u>

The mixture of elements of the struggle with participants in the demonstration will give the appearance of a spontaneous demonstration, lacking direction, which will be used by the agitators of the struggle to control the behavior of the masses.

7. <u>Conclusion</u>

Too often we see guerrilla warfare only from the point of

view of combat actions. This view is erroneous and extremely dangerous. Combat actions are not the key to victory in guerrilla warfare but rather form part of one of the six basic efforts. There is no priority in any of the efforts, but rather they should progress in a parallel manner.

The emphasis or exclusion of any of these efforts could bring about serious difficulties, and in the worst of cases, even failure. The history of revolutionary wars has shown this truth.

APPENDIX: SPEECH TECHNIQUES

1. <u>General Information</u>

The purpose of this appendix is to complement the guidelines and recommendations to the propagandist-guerrillas expressed under the topic of "Techniques of Persuasion in Talks and Speeches" (Section IV), in order to improve the capabilities for organizations and expression of thought on the part of those who wish to perfect their oratorical skills.

After all, oratory is one of the most valuable resources for exercising leadership. Oratory can be used, then, as an extraordinary political tool.

2. <u>The Audience</u>

Oratory is the coincidental means of communication par excellence; that is, the speaker and his audience coincide in a single time and place. For that reason, each speech should be a different experience, framed in "that" circumstance or actual situation in which the audience is living and by which it is influenced. So the audience should be considered as a "state of mind". Happiness, sadness, anger, fear, etc., are psychic states that we should consider to exist in our audience, and it is the environment that affects the target public.

The human being consists of a mind and a soul; he acts in accordance with thoughts and feelings, and responds to the stimuli of ideas and emotions. Therefore, there are only two possible approaches to any exposition, including speeches: a real approach, based on appeals to reason, that is, to thought; and an idealized approach, which appeals to the emotions, or to the sentiments.

As far as the speaker is concerned, even though he should be sensitive to the existing collective emotions, at the same time he should set himself apart in order to be able to effectively lead and control the emotions of the audience. When during the oratorical momentum the antithesis between heart and mind is produced, judgment, the characteristic of a leader, must always prevail.

3. Political Oratory

Political oratory is one of various forms of public speaking and usually accomplishes one of the following three objectives: it teaches, persuades or moves the audience; the method used boils down to appeals, commands, questions and answers.

Oratory is a quality so tied to political leadership that it can be said that the history of political speakers is the political history of humanity, a statement upheld by names such as Cicero, Demosthenes, Dante, Mirabeau, Robespierre, Clemenceau, Lenin, Trotsky, Mussolini, Hitler, Roosevelt, etc.

4. <u>Positive Aspects of a Speech</u>

In general the features most valued in a speech, and specifically in a political speech within the framework of psychological action in the armed struggle, are the following:

- **Brevity and succinctness**: a five minute speech is ideal. A speaker who is brief demonstrates even more his ability as stated in that well-known expression: "if they want a two hour speech, I'll begin now; if they want one that lasts only two minutes, let me think awhile".

- **Development around a theme**: a speech must be a group of organized ideas which develop around a subject. A good speech is expressed in concepts and not only with words.

- **Logic**: the ideas presented must be logical and easily acceptable. Never should the logic in the minds of the audience be challenged, since this would lead immediately to a loss of what is most important: namely credibility. When possible it is advisable to base a speech on a syllogism which the speaker should adapt to his exposition. For example: "Those who enrich themselves while governing are thieves; the Sandinists have become rich while governing; therefore, the Sandinists are thieves". This could be the message of a speech on the administrative corruption of the regime. Whenever a speech lacks an idea or a group of directing ideas, it can easily become dispersed and confusing.

5. <u>Parts of a Speech</u>

There is no true improvisation in oratory. Every speaker uses a "mental plan" which permits him to organize his ideas and concepts quickly. With practice it is possible to do this in only a few seconds, almost simultaneously with speaking.

The elements which constitute a speech appear below in the order recommended to those who wish to consistently improve their speaking ability:

– **Introduction of exordium**: Upon initial contact with the audience, a personal introduction can be made or one for the group to which we belong as well as the reason for our presence there, etc. During these first seconds it is important to make an impact, calling for the attention and arousing the audience's interest. For that there are resources like starting with key quotation or slogans previously arranged to tell a dramatic or humoristic anecdote, etc.

- **Proposal or statement**: the subject of the speech is defined, either by explaining it as a whole or in parts.

- **Assessment or argument**: arguments are presented in exactly this order: first the negative arguments, or those which oppose the thesis which is to be upheld, and then the positive arguments, or those favorable to our thesis, immediately adding proofs or facts which support these arguments.

- **Summing-up or conclusion**: a brief summary should be made and the conclusions should be made more explicit.

- **Exhortation**: an appeal for public action is made. In other words, the audience is encouraged almost always energetically to do or not to do something.

6. <u>Some Literary Resources</u>

Although there are typically oratorical figures of speech, truly, oratory has borrowed a large number of figures from other literary genres, several of which we use, often unconsciously, in our daily expressions and even in our speech.

Below we list a good number of literary figures which are frequently used in oratory, recommending to those interested that they use them in moderation, since an orator who makes excessive use of literary figures loses authenticity and sounds false.

The figures that are most often used in oratory are those obtained through the repetition of words at certain points of the speech, such as:

- **Anaphora** or **repetition of a word** at the beginning of each phrase. For example: "Freedom for the poor, freedom for the rich, freedom for all". In reiteration, a complete phrase (slogan) is repeated insistently throughout the speech. For example: "With God and patriotism we will defeat communism, because..."

- **Conversion** is repetition at the end of each phrase. For example: "The Sandinist [movement] pretends to be above everyone, dominate everyone, lord over everyone, and as an absolute tyranny, eliminate everyone".

- **Complexity**: repetition that takes place at the beginning and at the end of the clauses. Example: "Who brought the Russian-Cuban intervention? The Sandinists. And who trades in arms with the neighboring countries? The Sandinists. And who proclaims now to be a supporter of non-intervention? The Sandinists".

- **Reduplication**, when the phrase begins with the same word that ends the previous phrase. Example: "We fight for democracy, democracy and social justice". Linking is a chain formed by several duplications. Example: "Communism transmits the deception from the child to the youth, from the youth to the adult, and from the adult to the elderly".

- In the **play on words** one uses the same words with a different meaning to obtain a clever effect. Example: "The greatest wealth of each human being is his own freedom, because slaves will always be poor, but we the poor can have the wealth of our freedom".

- Similar **rhytm**, by using verbs of the same tense and person, or nouns of the same number and case. Example: "We who are fighting will enter marching because who perseveres reaches and who gives up falls behind".

- **Synonymity**, the repetition of words of similar meaning. Example: "We demand a Nicaragua for all without exceptions without omissions".

Among the most commonly used background figures of speech are:

- **Comparison or simile** which determines the resemblance relation between two or more beings or things. Example: "Because we love Christ, we love his bishops and ministers", "Free as a bird".

– **Antithesis** is the contrast of words, ideas or phrases of opposite meaning. Example: "They promised freedom and gave slavery; that they would distribute wealth and distributed poverty; that they would bring peace and brought about war".

Among the logical figures are the following:

– **Concession**, which is a clever way of conceding something to the opponent in order to better emphasize the difficulties by using conjunctions such as: but, however, although, nevertheless, in spite of, etc. Example: "The mayor has been honest here, but he is not the one who handles all the monies of the nation". This is an effective way of rebutting when the opinion of the audience is not completely on our side.

– **Permission**, when apparently one agrees to something but in reality rejects it. Example: "Do not protest but subvert", "speak low but tell everyone".

– **Prolepsis** is a refutation in advance. Example: "Some will think it is only promises; they will say just like the others said it, but it is not so. We are different, we are Christians, we consider God witness of our works".

– **Preterition** consists of a ruse which by feigning discretion; something very clear and indiscrete is said.

Example: "If I were not obligated to safeguard military secrets, I would tell all of you about the great quantity of armaments in our possession, so that you may have greater confidence in the certainty of our victory".

- **Communication** is a way of asking and answering a question oneself. Example: "If they have disrespect for God's ministries, will they respect us, simple citizens that we are? Never".

- **Doubt** is a way to express perplexity or helplessness in saying something, used solely as an oratorical aid. Example: "I am only a peasant and can tell you very little. I don't know very much and cannot explain the complex issues of politics. This is why I'm speaking to you from the heart, my simple heart as a peasant, which we all are".

- **Litotes** is a means of signifying much while saying very little. Example: "The nine commanders haven't stolen much, only the whole country".

- **Irony** consists of meaning the exact opposite of what is being said. Example: "The divine throngs who threaten and kill, those are really Christian".

- **Amplification** is presenting an idea from different angles. Example: "Political votes are the power of the people in democracy. Economic votes are their power in the economy. The majorities decide what is to be produced whether they buy or not. That is the way of economic democracy".

The pathetic figures most commonly used are:

- **Prayer or supplication** to obtain something. Example: "Lord, free us from the yoke, grants us freedom".

- The **implication of threat**, expressing a feeling against what is unjust or unsolvable. Example: "May there be a Fatherland for all, or for none at all".

- The **threat**, similar to the above, presents a feeling of ill-will towards others. Example: "May they sink into the chasm of their own corruption".

- The **apostrophe** consists of addressing something extraterrestrial or inanimate as if it were a living being. Example: "Mountains of Nicaragua, make the seed of liberty grow".

- **Interrogation** consists of questioning oneself for the sake of emphasis. It differs from the communication in that the latter gives an answer which is logical, not pathetical. Example: "If they have already killed my family, friends, my brother peasant, do I have another recourse but to take up arms?".

- **Insinuation** consists of intentionally presenting an incomplete thought to be completed mentally by the audience. Example: "They promised political pluralism and delivered totalitarianism; they promised social justice and they have increased poverty. They offered press freedom and delivered censorship. Now they promise the world free elections...".

Taiwan Says It Did Provide Aid to Contras, Los Angeles Times, May 16, 1987.

Anderson, Jack; Van Atta, Dale; *Red China Sell Arms to Contras*, The Washington Post, May 5, 1986.

Marshall, Jonathan, *Israel, the Contras and the North Trial*, MERIP, September/October 1989.

McManus, Doyle, *Contras May Have Got $30 Million From Saudi Arabia*, Los Angeles Times, January 15, 1987.

Pietrobon, Emanuel; *L'arte della guerra ibrida. Teoria e prassi della destabilizzazione*, Castelvecchi, 2022.

Acronyms

CDS: Comités de Defensa Sandinista.

CIA: Central Intelligence Agency.

EPA: Equipos de Propaganda Armada.

FSLN: Frente Sandinista de Liberación Nacional.

HUK: Hukbong Bayan Laban sa Hapo.

The written accounts of the CIA's subversive operations in Nicaragua during the 1980s do not end with the manual you have just finished reading.

This concluding section is designed to aggregate other important, though less well-known, documents from the United States' covert war against the Sandinistas, such as declassified reports and original language propaganda materials.

Contras plan powerful radio broadcasts into Nicaragua

By Marjorie Miller
Los Angeles Times

MIAMI — U.S.-backed Nicaraguan rebels soon will launch a powerful clandestine radio broadcast to try to fuel public discontent with Nicaragua's ruling Sandinistas and win popular support inside the country.

The 50,000-watt broadcasting station, apparently the world's only AM guerrilla radio channel, would be the Nicaraguan contras' biggest effort yet in the war's political side, which they have largely ignored until now.

"I think the radio is as important as the [insurgent] army," rebel spokesman Leonardo Somarriba said. "It is the tool we can use to get to the people's minds."

Radio Liberacion, as it is named, is expected to be on the air by the first of the year, Somarriba said. The 6 p.m.-to-6 a.m. broadcasts are expected to include anti-Sandinista music, soap operas, editorials and commentary by rebel leaders.

Productions already prepared include mocking characterizations of President Daniel Ortega and Interior Minister Tomas Borge speaking in the countryside, with sound effects of barking dogs, crowing roosters and piano scales for drama.

The polished programs have high-tech lead-ins with beeping radio signals and canned applause. And always the rebels' message: "Radio Liberacion . . . the voice of those who have no voice. . . . Thousands of compatriots who form the commandos of liberty in a country oppressed by international communism through nine traitors of the Sandinista front. . . . Communists — enemies of God and man."

Rebel leaders said their news programs would be "objective, without propaganda and without censorship," in an effort to earn them credibility and a wide audience and to counter the Sandinista-controlled media in Nicaragua.

"We want to be the number-one radio station in Nicaragua," said Frank Arana, a rebel spokesman.

U.S. officials who asked not to be identified said that the rebel radio would be broadcast from nearby El Salvador, where a leftist guerrilla movement is fighting to oust the U.S.-backed government. Contra sources said only that the transmitter "could be anywhere" and would not comment further.

The Salvadoran guerrillas receive assistance for their clandestine Radio Venceremos from Nicaragua. Contra leaders said that they had studied Venceremos as well as the U.S. government's Spanish-language Radio Marti, which is beamed at Cuba.

Radio is the most popular medium in poor countries such as Nicaragua and El Salvador, where television is expensive and illiteracy is high. Radio has been used extensively for "psychological operations" in the Salvadoran government's counterinsurgency war.

Contra spokesmen said that funding for the radio station did not come out of the $100 million in aid that Congress approved for the contras this year. However, the spokesmen would not identify the source or quantity of the "private donations" that they said were supporting the radio.

U.S. sources say that State Department and Central Intelligence Agency officials have advised the rebels on the radio, but contra spokesmen would not comment on whether they received any assistance. Regional political analysts have said that one of the contras' major problems was their lack of a political program and internal propaganda.

"They should have done this a long time ago," said a U.S. official who asked not to be identified. "They have got to get their message to the population. They have got to articulate what this war is about."

With the radio, the contras hope to increase the name recognition of their leaders, many of whom are little-known inside Nicaragua. They hope to convince Nicaraguans that they are a nationalistic movement — rather than a U.S. mercenary force, as the Sandinistas portray them in the state-run media — and to show that they are united.

The radio will be run under the name of the United Nicaraguan Opposition, the rebel's umbrella group. The Nicaraguan Democratic Force, the largest armed group, has had a weaker shortwave radio called 15 de Septiembre, which aired two hours daily but was hard to receive.

Sandinista spokesmen could not be reached for official comment on the radio, but a Defense Ministry official said, "First, let's see if they get it on the air, and then we'll worry about jamming it."

Misleading Americans

The Washington Post
The New York Times
The Washington Times
The Wall Street Journal
The Christian Science Monitor
New York Daily News
USA Today
The Chicago Tribune

L.A. TIMES, PT. 5, Pg. 1
Date *11 SEP 1988*

By Robert Parry and Peter Kornbluh

WASHINGTON

If George Bush has his way, the Iran-Contra affair will be the forgotten issue of the fall campaign. The vice president's men feel Bush has artfully dodged questions about his role while relying on press and public boredom to bury the issue once and for all. But now a troubling new question rises: What did Bush know about a covert White House propaganda bureaucracy that sought to manipulate the American public, Congress and the news media in support of Contra military aid?

The question could be difficult because it recalls the darker side of the Central Intelligence Agency, the outfit Bush once headed. According to documents unearthed by the congressional Iran-Contra committee, the domestic campaign, directed out of the National Security Council, was crafted by a senior CIA propaganda veteran and was staffed, in part, by U.S. Army psychological warfare specialists. Ultimately, it came to resemble the sort of covert political operation the CIA is allowed to run against hostile forces overseas but is forbidden from conducting at home.

Last year, as the Iran-Contra committee was writing its report, House investigators drafted a chapter on the domestic operation. It said that the propaganda campaign had used "one of the CIA's most senior specialists, sent to the NSC by Bill Casey [the late CIA director William J. Casey], to create and coordinate an interagency public diplomacy mechanism. [This network] did what a covert CIA operation in a foreign country might do—attempted to manipulate the media, the Congress and public opinion to support Reagan Administration policies. The problem with all this is—they tried to do it in America, to their own people, to their own Congress, to their own free press."

Inside the committee, the chapter's dramatic conclusion was hotly opposed by Republicans, who argued it was outside the panel's investigative mandate, and by some Democrats, who feared it would jeopardize support for the report's chief findings from moderate Senate Republi-

cans. In the rush to complete its work, the committee dropped the draft chapter, which was only recently obtained by the authors of this article.

Iran-Contra documents reflect three connections between the propaganda apparatus and the vice president:

—Bush's national security adviser, Donald P. Gregg, another ex-CIA hand, recommended CIA propaganda specialist Walter Raymond Jr. for the NSC staff in 1982, according to Raymond's deposition. With Casey's guidance and blessing, Raymond quickly assumed responsibility for creating a "public diplomacy" apparatus that employed overt and covert means to push for Contra aid.

—Bush, as a member of the NSC, would have had direct oversight of the public diplomacy machinery and, according to one document, favored its creation. In a 1986 memo to Casey, Raymond said the public diplomacy operation "reports directly to the NSC." Even budget and personnel questions were cleared through the NSC, according to Iran-Contra documents. After discussions at senior White House levels, President Reagan authorized creation of the public diplomacy bureaucracy in National Security Decision Directive 77, signed in January, 1983.

—A private arm of the propaganda apparatus planned to support Bush's 1988 presidential bid. In early 1986, Richard R. Miller and Carl R. (Spitz) Channell, who worked closely with Lt. Col. Oliver L. North, developed a pro-Bush program called "Future of Freedom Forums." One internal memo at Channell's National Endowment for the Preservation of Liberty said, "The vice president needs a vehicle which he can utilize to reach the high-dollar donors in the conservative ranks." It continued, "These donors perceive him as a liberal Republican unsure of himself and without determination to lead in tough circumstances." . In a Jan. 16, 1986, letter, Bush praised Channell's proposed forums as "of great interest to me, as well as to the President. My personal interest is such that I hope to be able to participate." But the forums never

110

came off. apparently because of scheduling problems

Although Administration public diplomacy participants defended their operation as a legitimate means of informing the American people, some voiced unease, in private, about its clandestine methods. In an interview, a senior NSC official acknowledged that the public diplomacy apparatus was modeled after CIA covert operations overseas: "They were trying to manipulate public opinion . . . using the tools of Walt Raymond's trade craft which he learned from his career in the CIA covert operation shop."

The suppressed Iran-Contra chapter argues that the propaganda bureaucracy behaved much like the secret Contra resupply operation—working out of the NSC to sidestep legal restrictions on the CIA. President Reagan's Executive Order 12333 bars the CIA from activities "intended to influence United States political processes, public opinion . . . or media."

Iran-Contra documents show that the public diplomacy campaign chief architects were Casey and Raymond. In his deposition to congressional investigators, Raymond defended his involvement, arguing that he officially retired from the CIA in April, 1983, so "there would be no contamination of this." In Casey's case, Raymond asserted that the director was participating "not so much in his CIA hat, but in his adviser to the President hat."

As the propaganda apparatus took shape in August, 1983, Casey summoned advertising specialists to the Old Executive Office Building to brainstorm selling a "new product—Central America—by generating interest across-the-spectrum," according to an NSC summary of the meeting. Sensitive to the prohibitions on executive-branch propaganda, Raymond noted in one August, 1983, memo that "the work done within the Administration has to, by definition, be at arms length." Raymond added that he hoped to keep Casey out of the loop.

Yet the documents show that Casey remained active through November, 1986, when the scandal broke. In a Sept. 13, 1986, message to North, then-National Security Adviser John M. Poindexter said Casey was pushing for a full-time White House specialist on Central America publicity: "I think what he really has in mind is a political operative that can twist arms and also run a high-powered public affairs campaign."

Working closely with Raymond, the Office of Public Diplomacy for Latin America and the Caribbean (S/LPD) became the most visible arm of the propaganda machinery. Created in July, 1983, S/LPD was housed at the State Department, but its director, Otto Reich, noted in one memo that the office "respond[s] to NSC direction." He explained that it was created because "the President, the vice president and others were, to say the least, very upset with the inability of the executive branch to publicly communicate with the American people" on what the United States was doing in Central America.

S/LPD generated one-sided publications on Nicaragua and El Salvador and pressured the news media to accept Reagan's stand on Central America. S/LPD employed Army psychological warfare specialists, such as Reich's executive assistant, Lt. Col. Daniel (Jake) Jacobowitz, and five Army experts from the 4th Psychological Operations Group at Fort Bragg, N.C., who were assigned to find "exploitable themes and trends."

In a legal opinion dated Sept. 30, 1987, the General Accounting Office, the congressional watchdog agency, sharply criticized the public-diplomacy office for sponsoring articles that were printed in leading newspapers under the names of presumably independent scholars. The GAO opinion said the articles amounted to "prohibited covert propaganda activities designed to influence the media and the public to support the Administration's Latin American policies."

The propaganda campaign also relied heavily on private-sector intermediaries to carry out activities that would otherwise violate laws against executive branch lobbying. According to the deleted Iran-Contra chapter, the propaganda bureaucracy "hired outside consultants, gave encouragement, support and direction to groups of private citizens outside the government who were undertaking efforts to raise money for Contra weapons, lobby the Congress and manipulate American public opinion and the media."

S/LPD was an important contact point for these efforts, directly employing a number of consultants who received no-bid contracts for lobbying and public relations in behalf of the Contras. Richard Miller's International Business Communications (IBC) received more than $440,000 in S/LPD contracts between 1984 and 1986, including a secret-classified $276,000 for such duties as monitoring media coverage of Central America.

IBC officials worked with North and Channell in placing pro-Contra advertisements in the districts of swing congressmen and hiring pro-Contra lobbyists. To raise money for these efforts, Reagan met personally with wealthy contributors who had given more than $300,000 and the President was enthusiastic about the efforts. The minutes of a

May, 1986, National Security Planning Group meeting record Reagan asking whether the private groups could do more.

What the propaganda apparatus did do was reshape the public debate on Nicaragua and pave the way for resumption of Contra aid in August, 1986.

"It is clear we would not have won the House vote," Raymond exulted in an Aug. 7 memo to Casey, "without the painstaking deliberative effort undertaken by many people in the government and outside."

The question for the vice president is whether he agrees that this was a legitimate use of government power.   □

Robert Parry is a national correspondent for Newsweek. Peter Kornbluh is an information analyst at the National Security Archive. This report adds new documentation to the authors' article for the fall issue of Foreign Policy; the views do not necessarily reflect those of the National Security Archive.

Zone Commander
COMANDANTE DE ZONA

Esto evita una reacción en
cadena, si cualquier célula es
infiltrada.

This avoids a chain reaction, should
any cell be infiltrated.

Líder de célula de
coordinación.
Coordination cell
leader

Miembro de célula de
coordinación.
Coordination cell
member

Líder de célula opera-
cional.
Operational cell
leader

Miembro de célula
operacional.
Operational cell
member

Línea de contacto y
conocimiento dentro
de la célula.
Line of contact a
acquaintance with
the cell

Línea de contacto y
conocimiento fuera de
célula.
Line of contact
acquaintance outs
the cell

61/62

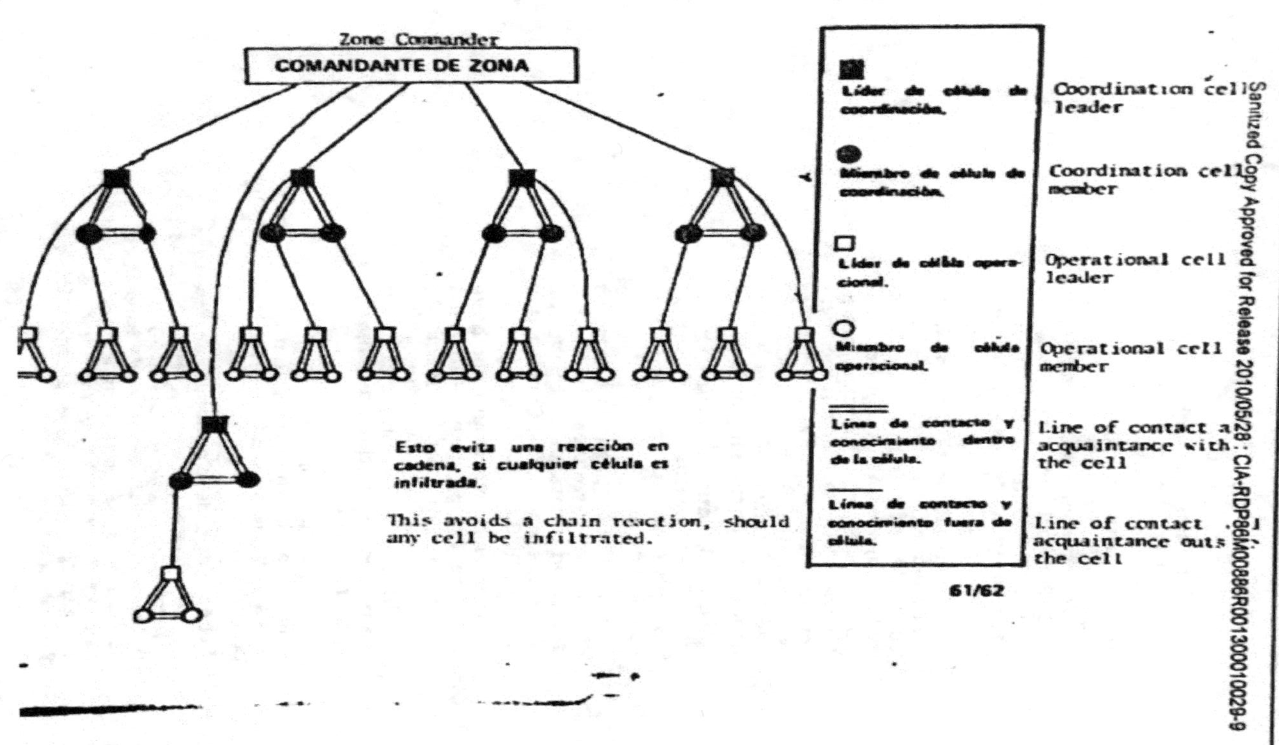

113

THE FREEDOM FIGHTER'S MANUAL

Practical guide to liberating Nicaragua from oppression and misery by paralyzing the military-industrial complex of the traitorous marxist state without having to use special tools and with minimal risk for the combatant.

NICARAGUAN PATRIOT:
TO SABOTAGE
THE MARXIST TYRANNY
IS TO VINDICATE
SANDINO'S MEMORY.
LONG LIVE FREE NICARAGUA!

"CIA Publishes Sabotage Manual...."

--Associated Press

WHAT THE FREE NICARAGUAN CAN DO
IN ORDER TO TIE DOWN THE MARXIST TYRANNY

All Nicaraguans who love their country and cherish liberty—men, women, young and old people, farmers and workers alike—surely ask themselves what they can do with the means at their disposal, in order to participate in the final battle against the usurpers of the authentic sandinista revolution for which the people of Nicaragua have fought and shed their blood for so many years. Some might think that today's armed struggle requires military supplies and economic resources only available to states or terrorist bands armed by Moscow. There is an essential economic infrastructure that any government needs to function, which can easily be disabled and even paralyzed without the use of armaments or costly and advanced equipment, with the small investment of resources and time.

The following pages present a series of useful sabotage techniques, the majority of which can be done with simple household tools such as scissors, empty bottles, screwdrivers, matches, etc. These measures are extremely safe and without risk for those who use them, as they do not require equipment, skill or specialized activities that can draw attention to the doer.

One combatant can perform many of them, without having to turn to collaborators or having to make a detailed plan beforehand. These are acts that can be done practically in an improvised way every time an occasion presents itself. Our sacred cause needs to have more men and women join its ranks in order to perform these sabotage tasks. However, necessary caution should be taken, and only when the task requires it, should another person or persons participate in or have knowledge of a given act. As mentioned above, the techniques found in this manual correspond to the stage of individual sabotage, or at the most cellular—with cells of no more than two individuals—of the clandestine struggle.

LO QUE EL NICARAGÜENSE LIBRE PUEDE HACER
PARA ATARLE LAS MANOS A LA TIRANA MARXISTA.

Todos los nicaragüenses amantes de su patria y de la libertad —hombres, mujeres, jóvenes, ancianos, campesinos y trabajadores— seguramente se preguntan qué pueden hacer con los medios que tienen a su alcance para participar en la batalla final contra la camarilla usurpadora de la auténtica revolución sandinista, por la que el pueblo de Nicaragua entero luchó y derramó su sangre durante tantos años. Se pensará que la lucha armada de hoy exige pertrechos y recursos económicos únicamente al alcance de los estados o las pandillas terroristas armadas y pagadas por Moscú. Pero hay toda una infraestructura económica esencial para que cualquier gobierno pueda funcionar que sí resulta fácil de trastornar y de paralizar incluso, sin valerse de armamentos ni equipos costosos y avanzados e invirtiendo sólo una proporción pequeña de recursos y tiempo.

Las páginas que siguen presentan una serie de sutiles técnicas de sabotaje que pueden aplicarse en su mayoría con simples herramientas caseras como son las tijeras, botellas vacías, destornilladores, fósforos, etc. Resultan además sumamente seguras para quien las aplica, pues no exigen equipos, adiestramiento o actividades especializadas que puedan llamar la atención. Un sólo combatiente puede aplicar muchas de ellas, sin tener que recurrir a colaboradores, ni trazar un plan muy detallado con anticipación. Son más bien golpes de mano que pueden consumarse de manera prácticamente imprevista cada vez que se presente una ocasión.

A nuestra sagrada causa le conviene, desde luego, ir sumando hombres y mujeres a las tareas del sabotaje. Pero ello debe hacerse con la debida cautela y sólo cuando la tarea entre manos exija que otra persona o personas participen en una acción determinada y que tengan por tanto conocimiento de ella. Como se indicó arriba, las técnicas expuestas en este manual corresponden a la etapa de sabotaje individual, o a lo sumo celular —con células de no más de dos individuos— de la lucha clandestina.

DON'T DO MAINTENANCE WORK
ON VEHICLES AND MACHINES

NO EFECTUAR LAS TAREAS
DE MANTENIMIENTO DE
VEHÍCULOS Y MÁQUINAS

EPS

ESCONDER Y
DAÑAR
HERRAMIENTAS
HIDE AND
DAMAGE TOOLS

ARROJAR HERRAMIENTAS POR
LAS ALCANTARILLAS

THROW TOOLS INTO SEWERS

LLEGAR TARDE
AL TRABAJO

COME LATE
TO WORK

DELAY IN
COMPLETING TASKS

DEMORAR EL
CUMPLIMIENTO
DE LAS
TAREAS

DECLARARSE ENFERMO
PARA NO
TRABAJAR

CALL IN SICK SO AS NOT TO WORK

DEJAR LAS LUCES ENCENDIDAS

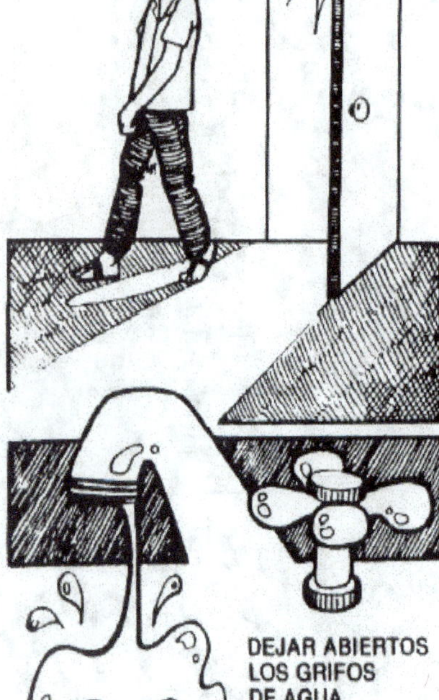

SEMBRAR FLORES EN
LAS GRANJAS DEL ESTADO

DEJAR ABIERTOS
LOS GRIFOS
DE AGUA

ACAPARAR
Y ROBAR
ALIMENTOS
DEL GOBIERNO

DISEMINAR RUMORES

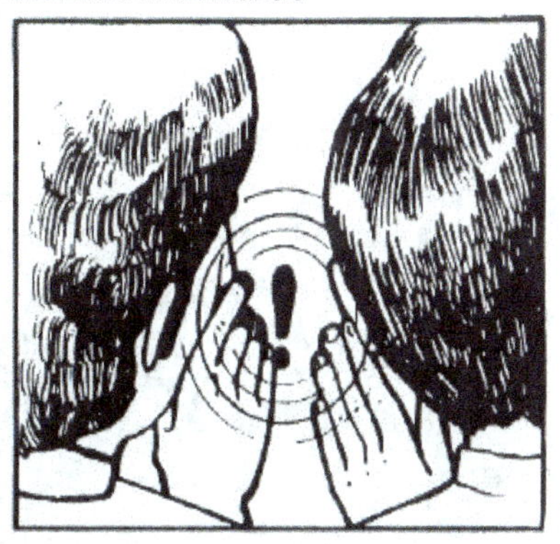

FSLN
COOPERATIVE

DEJAR
ABIERTOS
LOS CORRALES
DEL ESTADO

LEAVE OPEN THE
CORRAL GATES ON
STATE FARMS

TELEFONEAR HACIENDO
RESERVACIONES
FALSAS EN
HOTELES,
ETC.

TELEPHONE TO
MAKE FALSE HOTEL
RESERVATIONS, ETC.

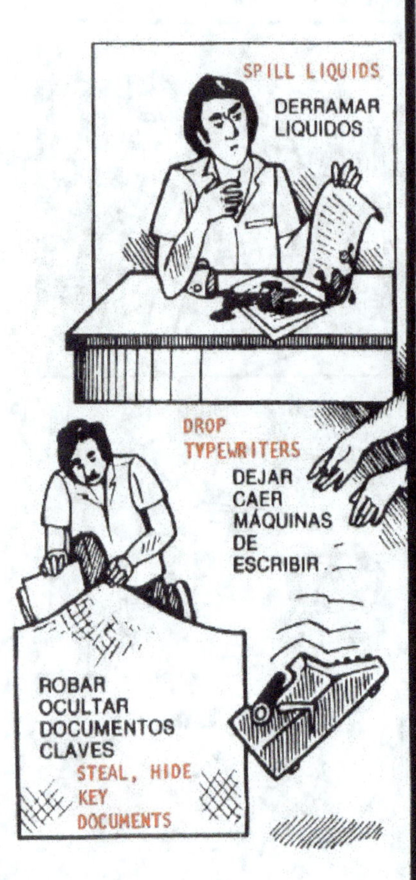
SPILL LIQUIDS
DERRAMAR LIQUIDOS
DROP TYPEWRITERS
DEJAR CAER MÁQUINAS DE ESCRIBIR
ROBAR OCULTAR DOCUMENTOS CLAVES
STEAL, HIDE KEY DOCUMENTS

THREATEN THE BOSS BY TELEPHONE
AMENAZAR AL JEFE POR TELÉFONO
TELEFONEAR DANDO FALSAS ALARMAS DE INCENDIOS Y DELITOS
TELEPHONE GIVING FALSE ALARMS OF FIRES AND CRIMES

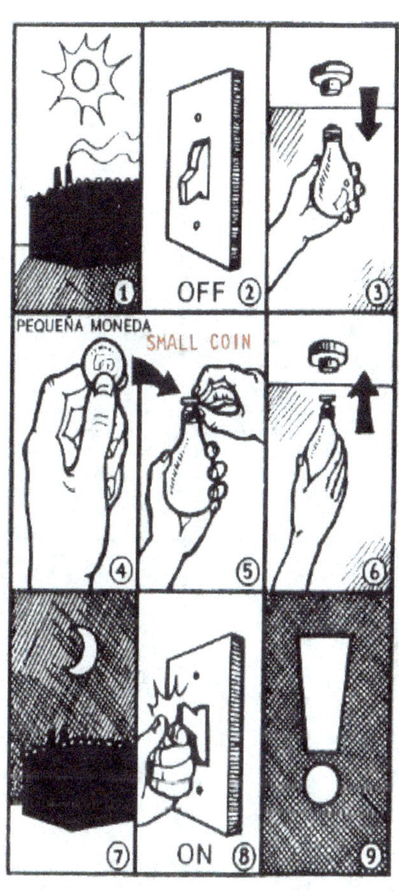
OFF
PEQUEÑA MONEDA
SMALL COIN
ON

DAMAGE BOOKS
DAÑAR LIBROS

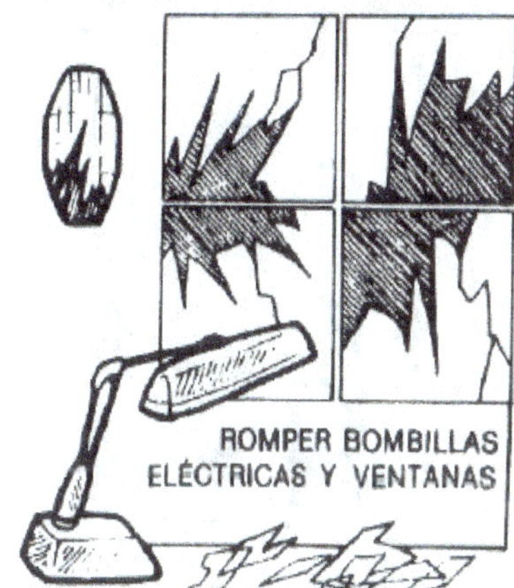
ROMPER BOMBILLAS
ELÉCTRICAS Y VENTANAS
BREAK LIGHT BULBS
AND WINDOWS

1. WET A SPONGE
2. WRAP THE SPONGE TIGHTLY
WITH A STRING AND LET IT DRY
3. REMOVE THE STRING
4. INTRODUCE THE SPONGE INTO
TOILETS OR WATER DRAINS TO STOP
THEM UP AS THE SPONGE SWELLS

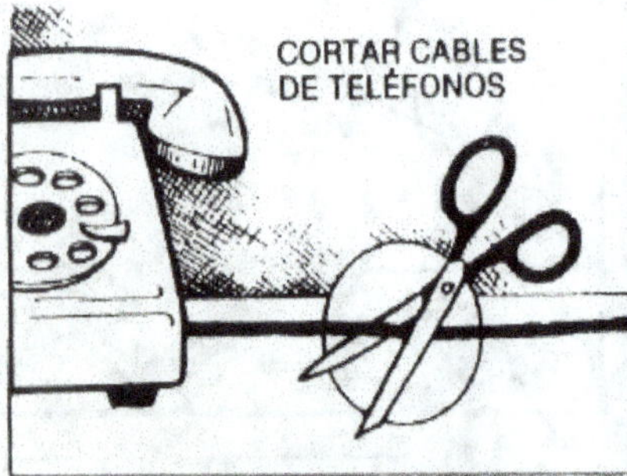

CUT THE
TELEPHONE CABLES
CORTAR CABLES
DE TELÉFONOS

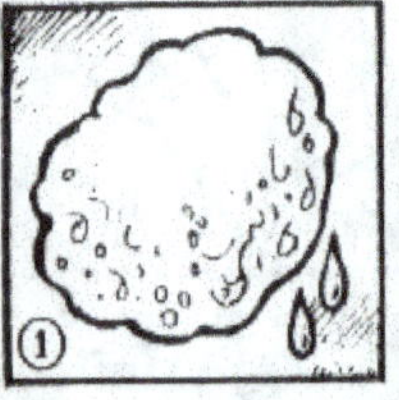

1. MOJAR UNA ESPONJA.
2. ENVOLVER LA ESPONJA BIEN APRETADA
CON UNA CUERDA Y DEJARLA SECAR.
3. REMOVER LA CUERDA.
4. INTRODUCIR LA ESPONJA EN CUALQUIER
INODORO O CONDUCTO DE DESAGUE,
PARA ASÍ OBSTRUIRLO AL HINCHARSE LA
ESPONJA

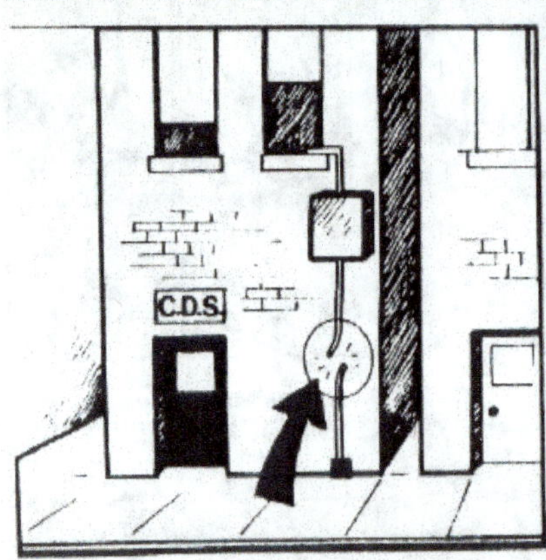

C.D.S.
CORTAR CABLE DEL
SISTEMA DE ALARMA
CUT CABLES OF ALARM SYSTEMS

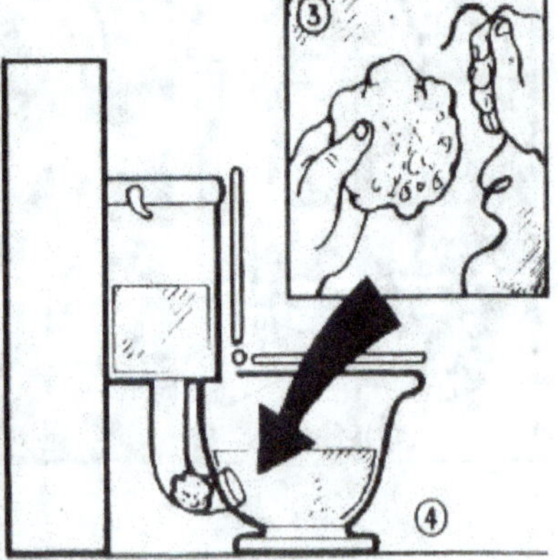

Nicaraguenses patrióticos pinten
sus gritos, quejas y demandas
contra los pro-Rusbanos del
FSLN en las paredes y otros
lugares para que todo el mundo
pueda ver su reacción al com-
unismo y los vendepatrias.

REGAR CLAVOS
EN LOS
CAMINOS Y
CARRETERAS

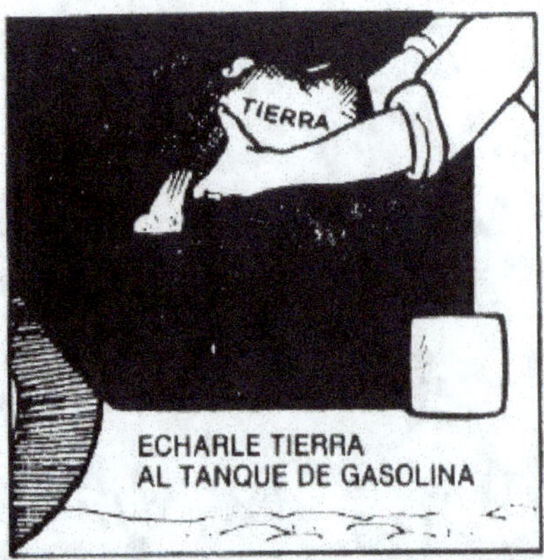
TIERRA
ECHARLE TIERRA
AL TANQUE DE GASOLINA

COLOCAR CLAVOS JUNTO A LOS
NEUMÁTICOS DE VEHÍCULOS
ESTACIONADOS

ECHAR AGUA EN EL TANQUE DE
GASOLINA
AGUA

123

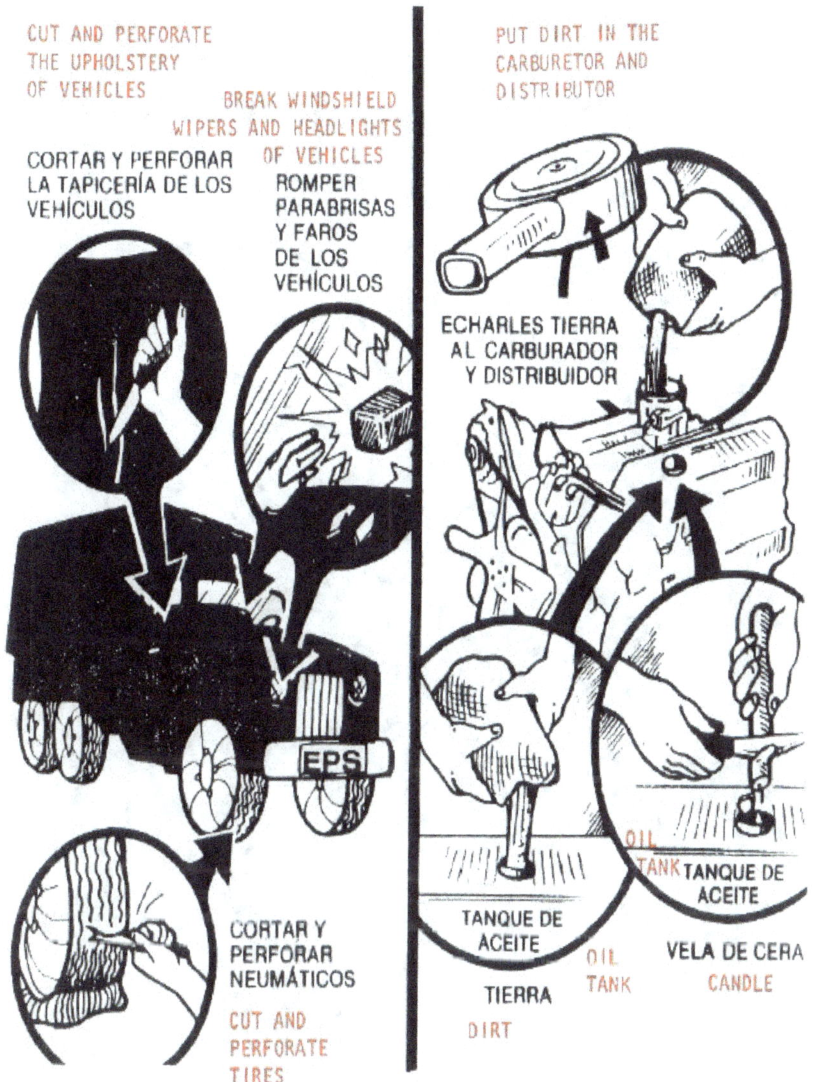

CUT AND PERFORATE
THE UPHOLSTERY
OF VEHICLES
CORTAR Y PERFORAR
LA TAPICERÍA DE LOS
VEHÍCULOS
BREAK WINDSHIELD
WIPERS AND HEADLIGHTS
OF VEHICLES
ROMPER
PARABRISAS
Y FAROS
DE LOS
VEHÍCULOS
PUT DIRT IN THE
CARBURETOR AND
DISTRIBUTOR
ECHARLES TIERRA
AL CARBURADOR
Y DISTRIBUIDOR
EPS
CORTAR Y
PERFORAR
NEUMÁTICOS
CUT AND
PERFORATE
TIRES
OIL
TANK
TANQUE DE
ACEITE
TANQUE DE
ACEITE
OIL
TANK
TIERRA
DIRT
VELA DE CERA
CANDLE

124

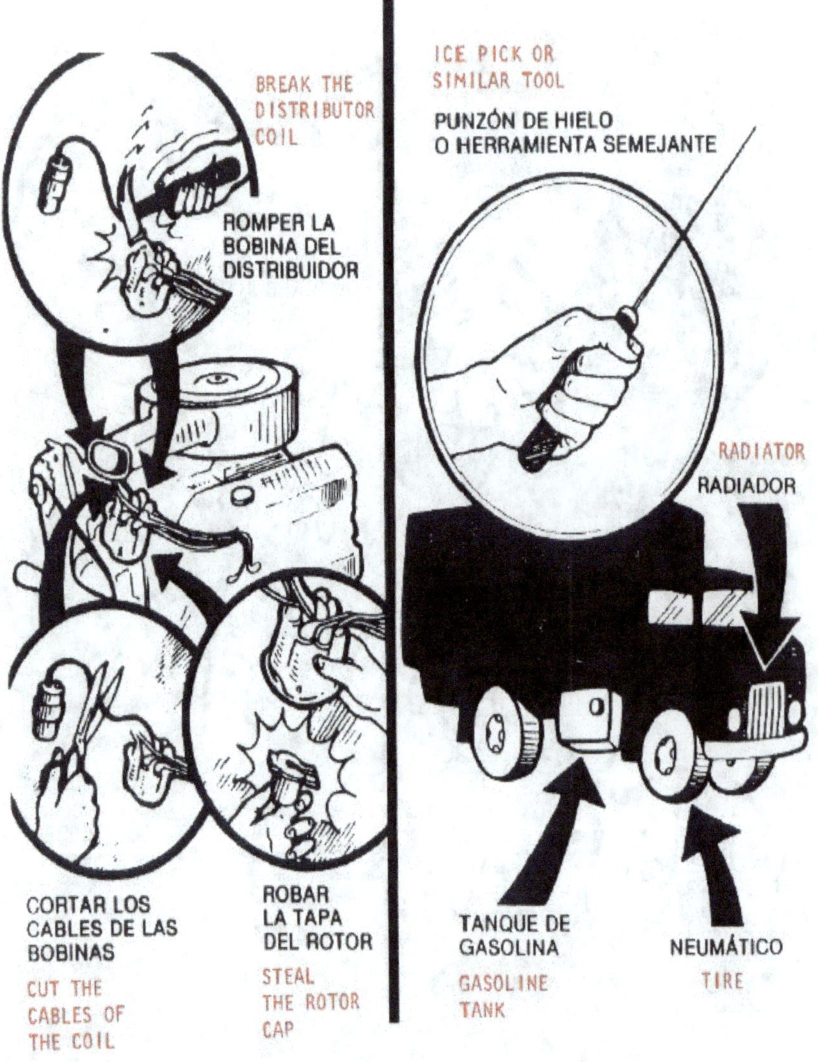

BREAK THE
DISTRIBUTOR
COIL
ROMPER LA
BOBINA DEL
DISTRIBUIDOR
ICE PICK OR
SIMILAR TOOL
PUNZÓN DE HIELO
O HERRAMIENTA SEMEJANTE
RADIATOR
RADIADOR
CORTAR LOS
CABLES DE LAS
BOBINAS
CUT THE
CABLES OF
THE COIL
ROBAR
LA TAPA
DEL ROTOR
STEAL
THE ROTOR
CAP
TANQUE DE
GASOLINA
GASOLINE
TANK
NEUMÁTICO
TIRE

PERFORATE BATTERY
CABLES

PERFORAR
LA CUBIERTA
DE LAS
BATERÍAS

INVERTIR LA
CONECCIÓN DE
LOS CABLES
EN LAS BATERÍAS

INVERT
BATTERY
CABLE
CONNECTIONS

ECHAR CLAVOS
EN LAS CÉLULAS
DE LAS BATERÍAS

PUT NAILS
IN BATTERY
CELLS

CUT DOWN TREES
OVER HIGHWAYS

DERRIBAR
ÁRBOLES
SOBRE LAS
CARRETERAS

COLOCAR
PIEDRAS
EN LAS
CARRETERAS
PUT ROCKS ON
THE HIGHWAYS

CARVAR ZANJAS
EN LAS CARRETERA

DIG DITCHES IN
THE HIGHWAYS

126

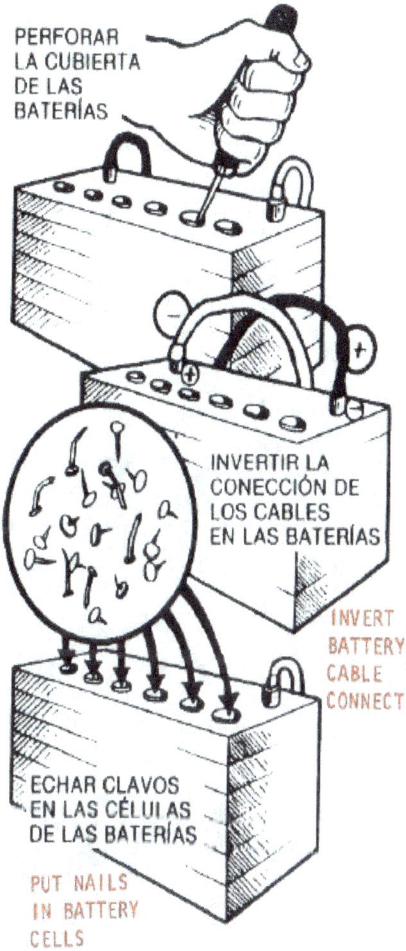

1. TWIST A STEEL BAR IN THE
FORM SHOWN IN THE DRAWING.
2. FASTEN THE TWO SECTIONS
TO JOIN THEM TOGETHER.
3. ATTACH A ROPE (NOT A
CABLE) TO THE HOOK IN THE
UPPER PART.

TORCER UNA VARILLA DE ACERO EN LA
FORMA QUE MUESTRA EL DIBUJO.

ATAR LAS DOS SECCIONES HASTA UNIRLAS.

ATAR UNA CUERDA (NO UN CABLE) AL GANCHO
DE LA PARTE SUPERIOR.

LANZAR EL GARFIO HASTA ENREDARLO EN
EL TENDIDO TELEFONICO (¡¡NUNCA CONTRA UN
TENDIDO ELÉCTRICO!!) Y TIRAR DE LA CUERDA
HASTA DERRIBARLO, COMO MUESTRA EL DIBUJO.

4. THROW THE GAFF UNTIL IT
CATCHES IN THE TELEPHONE
WIRES (NEVER IN ELECTRICAL
WIRES) AND PULL ON THE ROPES
UNTIL YOU BRING THEM DOWN AS
SHOWN IN THE DRAWING.

ARROW TO PERFORATE TIRES
1. USE A SHEET OF STEEL NO
LESS THAN 1.5 mm THICK AND
6.5 x 6.5 cm IN AREA.
2. CUT THE SHEET TO FORM
A TRIANGLE.

FLECHA PARA PERFORAR NEUMÁTICOS

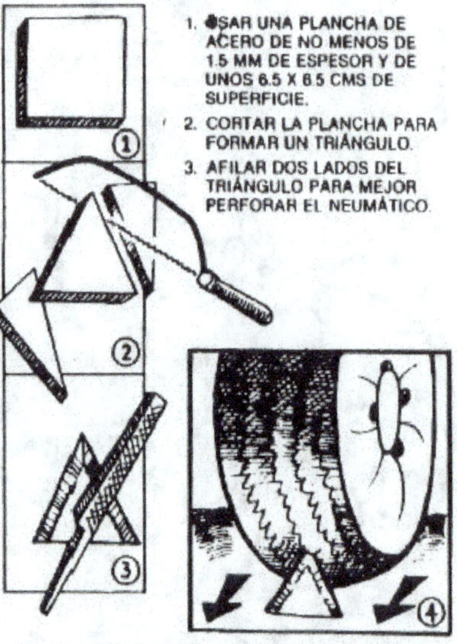

1. USAR UNA PLANCHA DE
ACERO DE NO MENOS DE
1.5 MM DE ESPESOR Y DE
UNOS 6.5 X 6.5 CMS DE
SUPERFICIE.

2. CORTAR LA PLANCHA PARA
FORMAR UN TRIÁNGULO.

3. AFILAR DOS LADOS DEL
TRIÁNGULO PARA MEJOR
PERFORAR EL NEUMÁTICO.

4. COLOCAR LA FLECHA ASÍ FORMADA SOBRE
EL SUELO, FIJANDO SU PUNTA AFILADA CONTRA
LA BANDA DE RODAMIENTO DEL NEUMÁTICO EN
UN ÁNGULO DE 45°. (GRADOS).

3. SHARPEN THE TWO SIDES
OF THE TRIANGLE TO BETTER
PERFORATE THE TIRE.
4. PLACE THE ARROW THUS
FASHIONED ON THE GROUND WITH
THE SHARPENED POINT ON THE
TIRE TREADS AT A 45° ANGLE

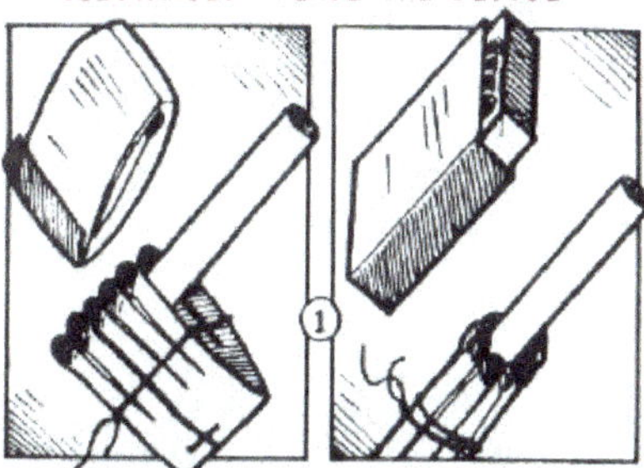

1. COLOCAR UN CIGARRILLO NO ENCENDIDO ENTRE AMBAS HILERAS DE FÓSFOROS. UNIRLOS FIRMEMENTE ATÁNDOLOS CON UNA CUERDA.

2. ENVOLVER LOS FÓSFOROS EN PAPEL SECO O CUALQUIER OTRA SUSTANCIA INFLAMABLE. COLOQUE EL DISPOSITIVO ENTRE CAJAS VACÍAS DE CARTÓN O MADERA.

3. ENCENDER EL CIGARRILLO POR SU EXTREMO LIBRE. LOS FÓSFOROS SE ENCENDERÁN EN 5 O 10 MINUTOS.

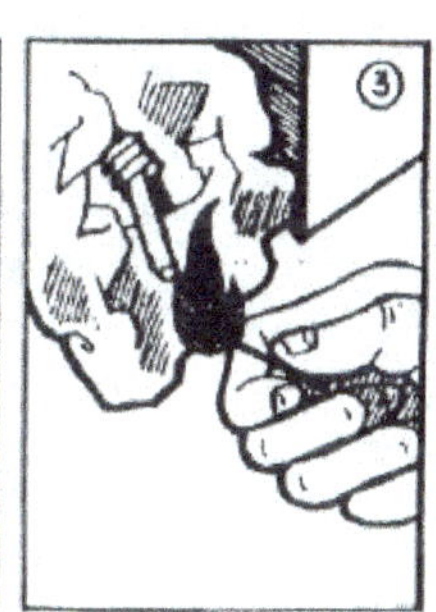

BOMBA INCENDIARIA ("COCTEL MOLOTOF")

1. LLENAR DE GASOLINA, LUZ BRILLANTE (KEROSÉN) O COMBUSTIBLE DIESEL UNA BOTELLA DE CUELLO ESTRECHO; MEJOR AUN SI SE LE AÑADE ASSERRÍN DE MADERA O JABÓN RAYADO.

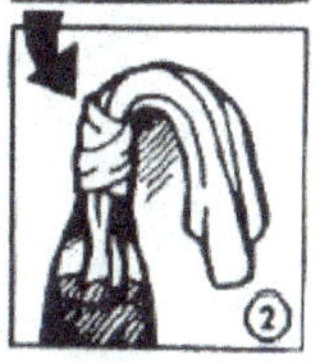

2. INTRODUCIR UN TRAPO EN LA BOTELLA HASTA QUE UN EXTREMO ROCE EL LÍQUIDO Y EL OTRO SE EXTIENDA NO MENOS DE 20 CMS DE LA BOCA DE LA BOTELLA. SELLAR FIRMEMENTE LA BOTELLA CON UNA CINTA O VENDA.

3. PARA ACTIVAR EL DISPOSITIVO:
   A) SOSTENER LA BOTELLA EN UNA MANO EXTENDIENDO BIEN EL BRAZO.
   B) ENCENDER CON LA OTRA MANO EL TRAPO.
   C) LANZAR INMEDIATAMENTE LA BOTELLA ENCENDIDA CONTRA EL OBJETIVO, CON FUERZA SUFICIENTE PARA QUE SE ROMPA AL HACER IMPACTO.

COPY _____ OF _______

12 March 1985

CONFIDENTIAL - SENSITIVE

PUBLIC DIPLOMACY ACTION PLAN
SUPPORT FOR THE WHITE HOUSE EDUCATIONAL CAMPAIGN

GOAL:

Congressional passage of aid to the Nicaraguan Freedom Fighters.

CENTRAL PERCEPTIONS

    PRIMARY PERCEPTION:
    -Vote for U.S. aid to the freedom fighters is a vital
national interest of the United States.

    SUPPORTING PERCEPTIONS:
            --U.S. history requires support to freedom fighters.
            --U.S. troops will eventually be required if aid is
            not given now.
            --Amount of aid is so miniscule that it hardly
            matters.
            --FSLN are puppets of Soviets
            --Nicaragua will become a Soviet military base if
            not resisted.
            --FSLN is racist and represses human rights.
            --FSLN is involved in U.S. drug problem.
            --FSLN are linked to worldwide terrorism.
            --FDN are freedom fighters.

    SPECIAL PERCEPTION:
            --Failure to vote for U.S. aid to the freedom
            fighters must be seen as a political liability.

IMPEDIMENTS:

    Situational:
            Deadline: Mid-April.
            Possible partisan response in House.
            Possible party-bolting in Senate
            Could be victim of budget cutting.
            Don't know what themes will cause Americans to share
            the administration's concern regarding Central
            America. (military build-up, communist threat on the
            continent drugs?)

<u>Perceptional</u>:
    Idea that U.S. Actions violate international law.
    Idea that U.S. actions preclude peaceful solutions
    in Central America
    Idea that aid to the Contras hurts "the moderates in
    Nicaragua.
    Idea that U.S. is "immoral" in supporting a covert
    action.

<u>ASSETS</u>:

--The Great Communicator.
    ---electoral mandate
--Respected key administration figures (Shultz,
Weinberger).
--Supportive private sector organizations.
--Some supportive congressmen.
--Historical U.S. policies
--Afghan precedent
--Cuban threat
--Some supportive media representatives.

<u>THEMES</u>:

-Overall theme: The Nicaraguan Freedom Fighters (FF) are
fighters for freedom in the American tradition, FSLN are evil.

-Major themes:

Freedom fighters are fighting democracy's battle.

    --Sub-themes: FSLN are outpost of the the Soviet
empire,
        ---Military build-up.
        ---Communist connection.
        ---The drug connection.
        ---Human rights violations:
            ----Freedom of the press.
            ----Right of assembly.
            ----Freedom of speech.
            ----Forced military conscription.
            ----Persecution of church groups.
            ----Destruction of the economy.

--Sub-themes; FDN are the good guys:
   ---FSLN goal is participation in an ongoing, viable democratic process, not fighting for "power-sharing."
   ---U.S. support for Contadora principles has not diminished.
   ---Central American democracies support our policies, and are worried that we will change them.
   ---Goal is to change Sandinista behavior; not overthrow them.
   ---FDN are the underdogs.
      ---- Anti-Somoza credentials.
      ---- Religious.
      ---- Anti-military.
      ---- Mostly poor peasants.
      ---- Poorly armed because of lack of U.S. support.
      ---- U.S. image will be destroyed if we sell out another ally
      ---- Thousands are joining resistance, despite its poverty of resources because it represents the ideals of the Nicaraguan people and their original goals in overthrowing Somoza

Subthemes; Regional geopolitics require defense of democracy in this hemisphere.

   -Soviets will view failure to support contras as license to move massively in CA.
     --Cam Ranh Bay Comparison
      ---U.S. Congress sold Vietnam out by failure to vote for ammo, Russkies moved into Cam Ranh Bay.
     --$14 million so small compared to U.S. budget, Soviets will believe that U.S. will pay no price no matter how obvious the threat.
     --West Coast surveillance
     --WWII Nazi sub-comparison
     --With control of Nu Soviets will be able to threaten both ends of Panama canal.

AUDIENCES:

   -U.S. Congress
   -U.S. Media
   -Interest groups

ACTIONS: (Related actions are listed under same key letter.
Subordinate actions are listed as numbered subset of a key
letter. Thus action A-1 must precede A-2. Actions in the B
series are independent of A series and can proceed
simultaneously. Completed actions are denoted by preceding $,
as $Z-2. New actions are designated by +, as +ZZ-1

   A. Johnathan Miller, John Blacken, John Scafe and Jake
   Jacobowitz will meet daily at 1800 to report progress,
   monitor progress, devise and revise themes and actions.
   Johnathan Miller retains overall control. (ASAP)

   B-1. Public opinion survey to see what turns Americans
   against Sandinistas (JS, to contact WH, results due by
   March 11).

   B-2. Review and restate themes in view of results of
   public opinion poll (JSM, JB, JJ, March 13).

   B-3. Prepare or assign articles directed to special
   interest groups at rate of one per week beginning Mar 4
   (examples: article on Nicaraguan educational system for
   NEA, article by retired military for Retired Officers
   Association, etc.] (JB, Mar 4 until vote)

   C-1. Assign knowledgeable person to prepare a complete
   list of publicly and privately expressed Congressional
   objections to voting for the aid. (Arturo Cruz, Jr., JSM
   to contact ASAP)

   C-2. Construct themes for approaches to Congressmen based
   on overall listed perceptions which will directly attack
   the reasons listed as above. (JSM, JB, JJ, ASAP upon
   completion of survey of Congressional objections)

   C-3. Presidential breakfasts, lunches, WHSR meetings and
   Camp David meetings with key Congressional leaders. (WH,
   Mar 24 until vote)

   C-4. President call key congressmen. (WH, two days before
   vote)

   D-1. Insure NSC details U.S. intelligence agencies to
   research, report to S/LPD, and clear for public release
   all Sandinista military actions violating Geneva
   Convention/civilized standards of warfare. (JJ to draft
   memo from Walt Raymond to community, Feb 26)

E. Update Green Book; send to congressmen, media outlets,
private organizations and individuals interested in
Nicaragua. (LT, DR, JB, Mar 25)

F. Release report on Soviet Military Build-up in Central
America and the Caribbean (LT, KS of DOD, Mar. 25)

G. Release paper on Nicaraguan media manipulation (JJ,
March 15).

H. Have a geopolitical paper written by Zbigniew
Brzezinski that points out geopolitical consequences of
Communist domination of Nicaragua (JJ contacted CM by Feb
28, CM will contact Zbig, plus Shlesinger, Jim Woolsey,
and Frank Cramer by Mar 4. S/LPD to prepare dummies for
edit--assignment not yet made, paper due by Mar 20)

I-1. H and ARA prepare a list of key congressmen
interested in Nicaragua. (JSM to contact H and ARA ASAP,
Mar 1)

I-2. Briefings on Nicaragua for Congressional staffers.
North on NU aggression and external involvement, Burghardt
on diplomatic situation. (WH, Mar 3-9)

I-3. Briefings in OEOB for members/Senators: Shultz,
McFarlane, Gorman and Shlaudeman to brief (requires
General Gorman to be placed on contract (WH, Mar 10-23)

I-4. Induce a mixed friendly and unfriendly CODELS to
visit Nicaraguan refugee camps in Honduras and Costa Rica
(include visit to FF camp and hospital in Honduras)
accompanied by press (North, Fox, Holwill, JSM to contact,
April 1).

I-5. CODELS visit regional leaders of Central America.
Regional Leaders convey importance of resistance fighters
in NU (WH, during Easter Recess, Apr 4-14)

J-1. S/LPD and WH Media Relations prepare a list of key
media outlets interested in Central American issues,
including newspapers, radio and TV stations (including
SIN). Where possible identify specific editors,
commentators, talk shows, and columnists. (JanB, Mar 8)

J-2. Contact with key media outlets as identified above
(WH to contact Lew Lehrman, S/LPD, PA to support, ASAP and
continuing until vote)

$J-3. Send resource book on the Contadora process to
congressmen, media outlets, private organizations and
individuals interested in Nicaragua. (JC, JJ to check
status, Feb. 26)

$K-1. Encourage FDN to select articulate freedom fighters
with proven combat records and to make them available for
contact with U.S. media representatives. (GC contacted by
JJ Feb 26,)

K-2. Encourage U.S. media reporters to meet individual
FDN fighters with proven combat records and media appeal.
(GC contacted by JJ Feb 26)

L. Assign to other agencies drafting of one op-ed piece
per week for signature of Administration officials. WH
will specify theme and thrust for the op-ed and retain
final editorial rights. (Ongoing beginning week of Mar 4)

M-1. ARA, S/LPD, NSC draft talking points on aid to
Nicaraguan Freedom Fighters (JSM to contact asap, Mar 11).

M-2. ARA and PA call newspaper editorial boards and give
them background on the Nicaraguan Freedom Fighters. (JSM
to contact, Mar. 10)

N-1. WH, ARA, S/LPD, NSC provide H with a list of
Nicaraguan emigres and masked freedom fighters to serve as
potential witnesses to testify before hearings on aid to
Nicaraguan Freedom Fighters. (JSM to contact NSC, Mar. 15)

N-2. Contact eyewitnesses to see if they would testify
before Congress about their aborted attempts to deal with
the FSLN. (JJ contacted GC Feb 26, task deadline Mar. 15)

O. Draft and distribute a paper on why Nicaraguans flee
their country. (JS to contact Macias ASAP, paper due Mar
15)

P. Themes, publications, interviews, and taped programs
produced for this effort will be coordinated with USIA for
overseas distribution and programming to USIS audiences
overseas, particularly foreign media. (ongoing throughout
life of plan)

Q-1. Production and distribution of _La Prensa_ chronology
of FSLN harassment. (TS Mar 11)

Q-2. Narcotics involvement document (NN Mar 15)

134

Q-3. PA or S/LPD reprint 10,000 copies of Secretary
Shultz' speech at the Commonwealth Club of San Francisco
(JC, Mar 7)

Q-4. S/LPD prepare paper detailing history of FDN's
offers to negotiate with the FSLN (DR, Mar 11)

Q-3. Document outlining "72-hour Document" (JSM to decide
on contractor week of Feb 25. FG to contact week of Feb
25.)

Q-4. S/LPD request declassification of <u>Nicaragua's
Development as a Marxist-Leninist State</u> (U), by Linn
Poulsen (JJ, memo on OR's desk, Feb 28) and publish as
State Dept. document (MCE and TS Mar 15)

Q-5. S/LPD request Bernard Nietschmann to prepare or
revise prior paper on suppression of Indian by FSLN (JJ
Mar 1, paper deadline Mar 25)

R-1. Presidential report to Congress certifying reasons
for releasing funds to FF (WH Apr 8)

R-2. NSDD (NSC April 8)

R-3. Major Presidential speech on Central America Note:
S/LPD suggests mention of FSLN suppression of Blacks and
Indians(WH Apr 8)

+S-1. NSC task appropriate agencies to prepare a report
on the economic costs to the United States of a
Marxist/Leninist regime on the Central American Isthmus.
(S/LPD draft language for NSC memo, Feb. 26. NSC task
agencies by Mar. 5; reports due Mar. 31.)

+S-2. S/LPD consolidate replies to NSC tasker on economic
costs to U.S. of a Marxist/Leninist regime on the Central
American Isthmus; prepare and distribute. (Apr. 5)

ACTION PLAN HEADINGS

GOAL:

PSYCHOLOGICAL CLIMATE:

ASSUMPTIONS:

CENTRAL PERCEPTIONS:

IMPEDIMENTS:

ASSETS:

THEMES:

AUDIENCES:

ACTIONS:

Documentation:

TIMELINE:

CONFIDENTIAL - SENSITIVE
12 March 1985

(8)

Wang 0515D

28 February 1985 version DESTROY ALL EARLIER VERSIONS!

Drafted by J. Jacobowitz

Copy distribution: Copy 1--JSM
                         2--JS
                         3--OJR
                         4--JB
                         5--NSC(ON)
                         6--Jiffy
                         Original held by JJ

136